The Teen Trauma Journal

of related interest

My Life After Trauma Handbook
Surviving and Thriving Using Psychological Approaches
Bridie Gallagher, Sue Knowles, Reggie Worthington and Jade Baron
Illustrated by Chloe Collett
ISBN 978 1 83997 128 0
eISBN 978 1 83997 129 7
Part of the Handbooks *series*

My Anxiety Handbook
Getting Back on Track
Sue Knowles, Bridie Gallagher and Phoebe McEwen
Illustrated by Emmeline Pidgen
ISBN 978 1 78592 440 8
eISBN 978 1 78450 813 5
Part of the Handbooks *series*

Obsessive Compulsive Disorder Diary
A Self-Help Diary with CBT Activities to Challenge Your OCD
Charlotte Dennis
Foreword by Dr Amisa Jassi and Dr Zoe Kindynis
ISBN 978 1 78775 053 1
eISBN 978 1 78775 054 8

The ACT Workbook for Teens with OCD
Unhook Yourself and Live Life to the Full
Patricia Zurita Ona, Psy.D.
Illustrated by Louise Gardner
Foreword by Stuart Ralph
ISBN 978 1 78775 083 8
eISBN 978 1 78775 084 5

The Healthy Coping Colouring Book and Journal
Creative Activities to Help Manage Stress, Anxiety and Other Big Feelings
Pooky Knightsmith
Illustrated by Emily Hamilton
ISBN 978 1 78592 139 1
eISBN 978 1 78450 405 2

The Teen Trauma Journal

UNDERSTANDING THE PAST AND EMBRACING TOMORROW!

DR. LAURA STOKES

ILLUSTRATED BY MASHA PIMAS

Jessica Kingsley Publishers
London and Philadelphia

First published in Great Britain in 2023 by Jessica Kingsley Publishers
An imprint of Hodder & Stoughton Ltd
An Hachette Company

1

Content warning: This book mentions abuse, emotional abuse and self-harm.

A CIP catalogue record for this title is available from the British Library and the Library of Congress

ISBN 978 1 83997 221 8
eISBN 978 1 83997 222 5

Printed and bound in Great Britain by Bell & Bain Limited

Jessica Kingsley Publishers' policy is to use papers that are natural, renewable and recyclable
products and made from wood grown in sustainable forests. The logging and manufacturing
processes are expected to conform to the environmental regulations of the country of origin.

Jessica Kingsley Publishers
Carmelite House
50 Victoria Embankment
London EC4Y 0DZ

www.jkp.com

Contents

Letter to Reader

Hi there!

I'm so glad you are reading this – it's intended to be a journal, just for you.

I wrote this journal to help you learn about trauma and talk about what you learn with the people you are close to – so they can support you.

As a psychologist, I have read a lot of books that explain how early experiences affect young people but haven't read a book written for teens and young adults themselves. It seemed to be about time there was one, so here we are! I hope that you'll find this journal helpful in some way.

What will this journal do for me?

This journal is partly to help you understand how early relationships can influence how you might think and feel about yourself. But it's also about you right now and your amazing future!

In my work as a psychologist, I have been lucky to meet lots of courageous young people, and some of them have been through difficult early experiences.

Whilst difficult early experiences can be really challenging, they can also lead to you developing huge strengths, including being strong, caring, resilient and understanding towards others.

This journal is a space to notice all these strengths. It will help you to spot areas you want to work on or learn to do differently.

> ### Quick tip!
> The most helpful way to use this journal is to have a 'go-to' adult who you trust and you can talk to about it. The journal includes

emotional topics, and having the support of someone close will be helpful.

This person could be a parent, foster carer, aunt, social worker or residential carer – as long as they are someone you trust and feel safe with. There is a short letter written for this adult at the back of the journal.

If you have an idea of who you want to ask, show them this letter before you carry on with the journal.

What will the journal cover?

The journal includes chapters about relationships, emotions, thoughts, school and other areas.

There will be ideas that you'll find helpful and others that you won't – and that's fine. Each chapter has space for your own ideas about how it relates to you.

You will need to read Chapter 1 first. This is your starting point, your 'Level 1', and you need to complete it before you move on to the rest of the journal. It's like a practice mode in a video game, where you learn and master your new skills.

After Level 1, you could read this journal in the order it's written or skip to the chapters that spark your interest the most.

Taking care of yourself

Reading this journal may bring up some challenging 'stuff' – feelings, thoughts or memories. The first rule is to look after yourself.

Ways of looking after yourself include:

- making sure a trusted adult helps you to work through it
- only reading as much as you feel able to
- giving yourself regular breaks
- using the grounding activities when needed.

Remember to look at Chapter 1 before moving on with the rest of the journal; this will help you throughout.

More help

This journal is not intended to be a replacement for therapeutic support if that would be helpful.

If you need extra help as you are reading this, let someone know. That could be a family member, a professional or a trusted friend. There is information at the end of the journal about extra supports. You can also talk to your doctor – they will know about support in your local area.

Thank you for reading; I really hope you find this helpful in your life.

With warm wishes,

Laura

> You can write, scribble or draw in the journal – whatever makes it feel like it's yours! If you want to use any of the activities again, you can download and print off the full booklet of all pages marked with ★ at https://library.jkp.com/redeem using the code MZVSMRH

★ **MY JOURNAL PROGRESS**

As you work through sections, tick the boxes below to update your status bar, showing how much you have worked through. You can then write your top take-away for each section. You don't have to cover each section in order, but it will help you see how far you have come!

Coping Skills and Safety Anchors ☐ ....

About Me ☐ ....

Surviving and Thriving ☐ ....

Trauma Whistle-Stop Tour ☐ ....

Stories About Yourself ☐ ....

Compassion ☐ ....

Sleep ☐ ....

Eating and Movement ☐ ....

Attachments and Why They Are Important ☐ ....

Fight, Flight and Freeze (3 F) ☐ ....

Living With Strong Emotions ☐ ....

Emotions and Attachment ☐ ....

Anger ☐ ....

Worry ☐ ....

Shame and Guilt ☐ ....

Bullying Thoughts ☐ ....

Relationships (Getting an Updated Map!) ☐ ....

Unsticking Memories ☐ ....

Survival Strategies ☐ ....

School/College ☐ ....

Being Assertive ☐ ....

My Present and Future ☐ ....

CHAPTER 1

Coping Skills and Safety Anchors

Let's learn some coping skills before progressing to the next chapters.

These are called **safety anchors**. Like a ship with an anchor that keeps it safely in place so it doesn't float away, the anchors will keep you grounded in the present when needed. Practise these skills so they are ready to use whenever you need them, and come back to this section as often as you need to.

Have a doodle on the journal page, 'My safety page', at the end of this chapter, to help you think about where you feel safest and who with. This might tell you where you'd like to work through your journal and which person you'd like to help you do it.

Anchor 1: Practise a safe memory

Working through this journal may bring up difficult memories. Take a moment to remember a time you felt very safe before starting.

Really remember the details: where you were, what was around, what you could see, hear and smell, and how you felt. Once you've got it in mind, use the journal page, 'My safe memory', to draw or write things that quickly bring this memory to mind when you need it. You can return to this at any time while reading the journal.

Anchor 2: Ground yourself in the here and now (if that is safe)

If you've had upsetting experiences, it can be easy to get caught up in memories of these and find you've lost track of time and place. This might make it hard to distinguish between the past and present when under stress.

Bringing yourself back to the present calms your brain and body. You can do this by noticing what you can immediately touch, smell, see, hear and taste. Let's try it:

Close your eyes for a few seconds, take a deep breath and when you open your eyes, notice the following things:

- What can you see around you? Maybe the trees through the window, the colour of the wall.
- What can you feel or touch? Maybe the chair, the ground under your feet.
- What can you hear? Maybe a bird outside, a car engine.
- What can you smell? Maybe someone cooking dinner.
- What can you taste? Maybe your last cup of tea, a piece of chocolate.

This feedback from your senses reminds your brain and body that you are not in the past. Focus on 5, 4, 3, 2, 1:

Senses	Examples
5 things you can see	Bird outside, a tree, my fingerprint
4 things you can feel	Feet on the ground, tabletop, one young person said they really liked the feel of their ear lobe (Random! But no judgements here – whatever works for you)
3 things you can hear	Wind in the tree, traffic noise, birds chirping
2 things you can smell	Washing powder on clothes, perfume
1 thing that you can taste	Toothpaste from brushing teeth

Do this whenever you need to connect back to the present.

I was told to try focusing on my senses when I got overwhelmed. It seemed weird at first, but now I like it. It helps me get out of my head and back in the room. **Jamie, 14**

It's important to be able to do this technique anywhere, whether you are out in the park, at school or on holiday. You don't need any materials to do it, just your senses.

Some people also choose to make a sensory box, containing things they like to hear, see, smell, touch and taste. This box can be made and kept somewhere, ready for whenever you want to tune into your senses using things you really like. It could include your favourite essential oil or perfume, a soft fabric, earphones for music, a favourite photograph and a food you enjoy.

Anchor 3: Movement

Movement can help connect you with the present, whether it's walking, football, yoga, dance, press-ups, squats, star jumps, stretches or anything else you enjoy! Connecting to your body through **movement** is one of the fastest ways to stay in the present.

Anchor 4: Focusing on your breathing

When we're scared, our breathing quickens. This sends a signal to your body that you are under threat and increases feelings of fear. Breathe **slowly** and **deeply**, to calm your body. You can practise by using the finger breathing technique:

1. Stretch your hand out like a star. Get the pointer finger on your other hand ready to trace up and down your fingers.
2. Move up each finger slowly (breathing in), and then slide down the other side (breathing out).
3. Breathe in through your nose and out through your mouth.
4. Repeat until you feel more connected to your breathing, tracing your hand each time.

Alongside these four anchors, we can use two other strategies to help.

Accepting emotions

Note down any emotions that you experience while working through your journal. Instead of squeezing them out, make room for them in your body.

Think of emotions like a wave in the sea, coming and going.

They might feel stronger sometimes and then reduce again. Instead of forcing them away, allow yourself to feel your emotion and use one of your anchors (like breathing) alongside this.

Try not to increase the feeling you experience – just notice it and allow it to be there. Emotions are temporary and however strong they are, they will pass with time.

There's another way of thinking about this – let's move from the sea to the swimming pool!

Imagine you're in a pool with a blow-up beach ball. Now imagine this beach ball represents a difficult emotion. Sometimes we try and push the beach ball (difficult emotion) down, under the water, because we don't want to see it or deal with it. Now, we can just about manage to hold the beach ball under the water for a short time, but it takes a lot of effort and concentration and stops us from enjoying being in the pool. As soon as we take our eye off the ball for a few seconds, it pops up forcefully and causes a splash.

Emotions can be just like the beach ball, so instead of trying to push emotions down, try to let them float around and come in and out of your view. It's easier, it's less effort and you're less likely to get splashed!

Self-care
Make sure you are looking after yourself physically. This could be: allowing yourself enough time to sleep, exercising, doing activities you enjoy, spending time with people who are important to you and eating well.

Why do the ideas in this journal matter?
When we're calmer, it's easier to focus on positive things in our life, like:

- learning
- developing friendships
- enjoying hobbies.

Hopefully, using this journal will start conversations about important topics, allowing you to work through any difficult areas. You can then be freed up to focus on your life now and on the amazing times to come in your future!

Complete the journal page, 'My present moment', before you read more. You can then use this whenever you need to remind yourself you are safely in the present.

★ MY SAFETY PAGE

Where do I feel safest?	Where do I feel most relaxed?
My favourite things to have around me	**Who helps me to feel safe?**

★ MY SAFE MEMORY

Use this space to draw your favourite image to think about when you want to feel safe.

★ MY PRESENT MOMENT

The date is: . . . .

5 things I can see:

1. . . . .

2. . . . .

3. . . . .

4. . . . .

5. . . . .

4 things I can feel:

1. . . . .

2. . . . .

3. . . . .

4. . . . .

3 things I can smell:

1. . . . .

2. . . . .

3. . . . .

2 things I can hear:

1. . . . .

2. . . . .

1 thing I can taste:

1. . . . .

★ **SAFETY ANCHORS**

Remember, learning new skills, including safety anchors, takes practice. If they are not helpful at first, keep practising and get someone you trust to help. Keep a note of what works for you below.

Safety anchors and strategies that work for me

Safety anchor	Who can help me practise?	Helpful (yes/more practice needed)
Safe memory		
Grounding		
Movement		
Focus on breathing		
Accepting emotions		
Self-care		

CHAPTER 2

About Me

My team

We all need a team, whether it is in sports, work, school or our family!

This journal is best worked through with your team, so think whose support you need. It might be people you can talk to easily or someone who makes you laugh.

★ In the circles below, write or draw yourself in the middle one and put the people in your back-up team around you. Let them know you are working through this journal and will want their support. People in your team could be: family members, carers, friends, pets, a favourite teacher or anyone who you find a support.

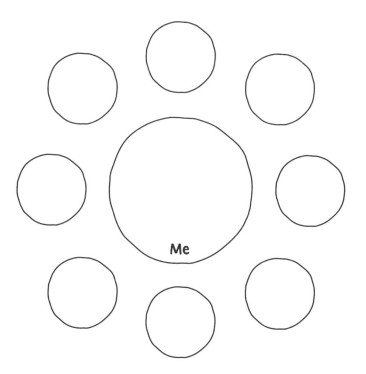

Me

It's not the number of people in your team that's important, it's about having one or two people you trust to help you.

Once you have written down who is in your team, talk to them about how they can help. This might include:

- setting a regular time to work through the journal with you
- talking about something unrelated to this journal
- watching a film together to distract you.

Your team might include professionals if you feel you need more help, like a health or social care professional, your GP, school nurse or social worker.

★ ALL ABOUT ME

We all have 'likes' – things that are important to us and things we are good at.
    These help make up who you are and can be useful to remember when you want to focus on your current life. Use the space below to make this journal your own.

Name/preferred name: . . . .

Age: . . . .

My identity is: . . . .

My hobbies: . . . .

Things I am good at: . . . .

My best memory: . . . .

Where I feel most relaxed: . . . .

People I feel most relaxed with: . . . .

Nice things my friend would say about me: . . . .

. . . .

My strengths: . . . .

People who are most important to me: . . . .

Animal friends/pets: . . . .

★ MY RELATIONSHIPS

We are important to lots of people in different ways. We might be a friend, step-sister, foster brother, nephew, girlfriend, son or adopted daughter. Tick all the roles that you hold.

Sister	☐	Stepdaughter	☐
Stepbrother	☐	Adoptive son	☐
Adoptive sister	☐	Grandchild	☐
Foster brother	☐	Cousin	☐
Adoptive daughter	☐	Girlfriend	☐
Nephew	☐	Stepson	☐
Daughter	☐	Foster daughter	☐
Adoptive brother	☐	Teammate	☐
Niece	☐	Friend	☐
Foster son	☐	Best friend	☐
Stepsister	☐	Aunt	☐
Brother	☐	Uncle	☐
Carer	☐	Son	☐
Foster sister	☐	Partner	☐
Boyfriend	☐	Student	☐

Other roles not listed:

. . . .

. . . .

. . . .

Future roles I might have:

. . . .

. . . .

. . . .

. . . .

. . . .

. . . .

CHAPTER 3

Surviving and Thriving

Your strengths

I've coped with some really tough things. When something comes along now, I think of all the things I've got through and how strong I am, then I know I'll be OK and that I don't have to cope on my own. **Ismail, 18**

If you are reading this, you have probably already got through tough times. Because you have coped with tough stuff in the past, you may be more resilient to future challenges. You will have developed your own personal strengths: 'I've coped with challenges and come out the other side.' Sometimes, when we keep struggling with things, we can start thinking 'What's wrong with me?' It can be helpful to balance these thoughts by also asking 'What's STRONG with me?'

★ Use the space below to think about challenges you have already overcome in your life.

Challenges I've overcome already:

....

....

....

....

....

....

Overcoming challenges can help people develop qualities that help them get through difficult times.

★ STRENGTHS I'VE DEVELOPED

Have you developed any of the strengths below? Circle any that fit for you. If you are not sure, ask someone else what they think.

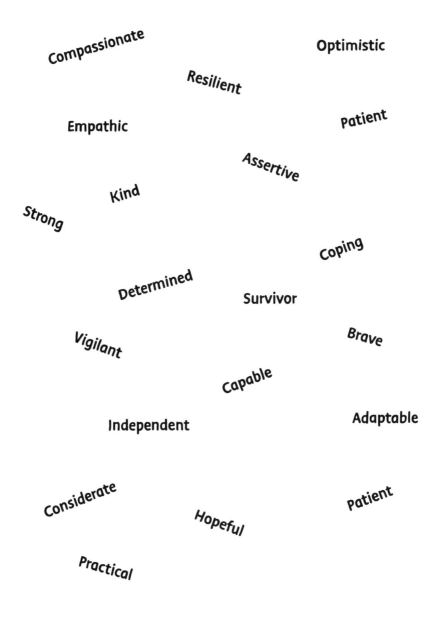

Compassionate

Optimistic

Resilient

Empathic

Patient

Assertive

Kind

Strong

Coping

Determined

Survivor

Vigilant

Brave

Capable

Independent

Adaptable

Considerate

Patient

Hopeful

Practical

Kintsugi

See this pot? It's Japanese. When it was broken, the owner didn't throw it away, they repaired it. When they repaired it, they didn't hide the repairs. They made them with gold, so everyone could see the history of the pot. In Japanese culture, the break is part  of the **story** of the pot. After the break and repair, the pot is even more beautiful and stronger than it was before. The pot has survived, come back together and is **more than it was before**. This is called 'Kintsugi'.

In this way, past experiences are like the breaks where you have healed and become even stronger for it.

Thriving!

The really serious German philosopher Friedrich Nietzsche said 'That which does not kill you, makes you stronger.'

He meant that people can go through really hard things and come through – from victim to SURVIVOR and THRIVER! Remember, the future has loads of amazing possibilities, so even if things have been tough, it doesn't mean they always will be.

Being a survivor can push people to:

- learn about themselves
- grow
- change.

One way to think about it is 'If I've coped with all this, I can cope with anything!' Often, really inspiring people have been through really tough stuff!

Resilience isn't pretending things haven't been tough or don't hurt, or that you don't need help ever (we all do sometimes). Instead, it is acknowledging your strengths and what you have already got through.

It's important to know that resilience isn't something you either have or don't have; it can grow like a flower through a crack in concrete – anywhere and any time!

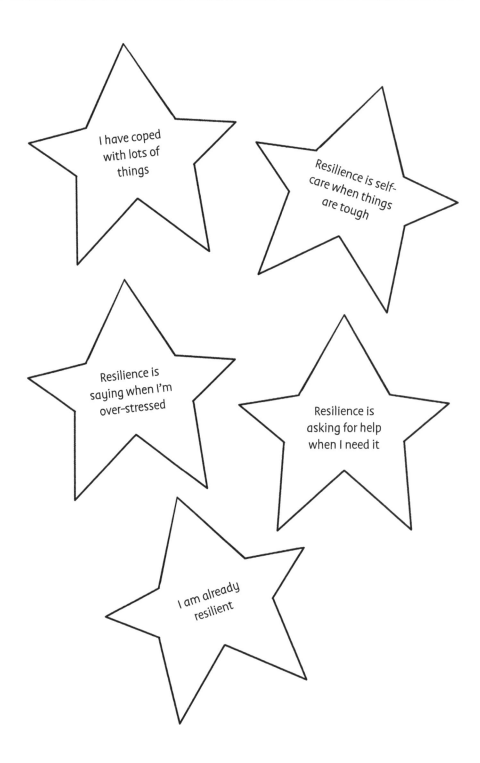

CHAPTER 4

Trauma Whistle-Stop Tour

Written with Dr. Ellen Westwood

This journal is called *The Teen Trauma Journal*, so let's talk about what 'trauma' means. You might want to involve someone supportive for this chapter. Someone who supported me with this topic was Dr. Ellen Westwood. Ellen is a psychologist too, and she helped by sharing her ideas and co-authoring this chapter.

What is trauma?

The word trauma is an 'umbrella term' – it is used to cover different things. It can be used to describe **traumatic experiences** (things that happen to someone) or the possible **after-effects** (the bodily, behavioural and emotional reactions that may happen following the traumatic experience).

The word trauma is used in different ways by different people – not so helpful when we are trying to explain it in simple terms! But let's have a go at considering what trauma means and what can cause it.

The word 'trauma' gets used in relation to an event or events that may be considered:

- frightening
- distressing
- shocking
- or even, life-threatening.

Trauma can result from someone:

- being harmed directly
- witnessing harm to someone else
- living in a traumatic environment.

Potentially traumatic events can leave someone with different experiences, such as feeling:

- under threat
- abandoned
- trapped
- powerless
- ashamed.

Everyone has different reactions to events that are potentially traumatic.

★   Time for a pause and doodle. Are there any surprises here? Where have you heard the word 'trauma' before? How do you understand the word?

How is trauma different to stress?

Everyone experiences stress in their life at some point. It might be about an exam, an argument or losing something...the list could go on!

Stress can be helpful, as it can motivate us to do things, like revise for an exam, apologize to a friend or search for the thing we lost. This type of stress is manageable and can be overcome without any negative effects.

People may experience trauma when the stress is unmanageable. This is sometimes called 'toxic stress'. This happens when experiences are frightening, repeated or prolonged and the person is unable to manage or escape the stress.

Childhood experiences

Traumatic experiences in childhood are different to traumatic experiences in adulthood, because children are less able to change their situation and their brains and bodies are still developing.

Potentially traumatic experiences in childhood are often called 'adverse childhood experiences', which can sometimes be shortened to 'ACEs'. Here is a list of what these experiences might include:

Violence

Witnessing violence between people or violence happening to you. Violence involves physical aggression or threats of physical force.

Abuse

There are different types of abuse: sexual, emotional and physical. This is where someone causes harm to another person.

Neglect

When things are not done for a growing child and this causes harm, like not getting enough food or not being supported to go to school.

Substance use

Growing up in a house where people are struggling with substance use – perhaps alcohol or drugs – can be an adverse experience depending on how it affects the person. For parents, it gets in the way of looking after their children and keeping them safe.

There will be many other really significant events that we have not listed here, including things like: separation from a parent (e.g., through death or a prison sentence), serious illness during childhood or significant parental mental health issues. It's important to remember that what is considered traumatic is really personal to each individual.

Reactions after adverse events

Reactions like sadness, confusion, upset, numbness or anger after a serious event are **normal responses** to upsetting experiences. These are natural things to feel after an extremely stressful situation.

It's important to allow yourself your own reaction if you have been in a very distressing situation. There's no right or wrong way to deal with it.

Single event or repeated traumatic experiences

The term 'traumatic experience' can refer to a single event (it happened once – like a car accident) or repeated events (these may have happened over weeks, months or years).

What might people notice if they've experienced trauma?

No two people are the same – even identical twins have different fingerprints! The impact that experiences can have on people varies.

Any and all reactions while in a distressing situation are valid – they are ways of coping. After a big event, the brain tries to make sense of what happened. Sometimes it can do this successfully and the upsetting feelings reduce over time (this might take a few months to happen naturally).

Other times, the brain may struggle to make sense of what has happened. A person may experience upsetting feelings and experiences for much longer. If these persist for a long time, they might be trauma symptoms.

Whether or not someone develops longer-term trauma symptoms can depend on lots of factors, including how much support they have had, when it happened and if they had a caring adult to support them at the time of the experience.

Some examples of things that people may notice after a traumatic experience are:

- not having the energy to do things they used to enjoy
- feeling jumpy and on edge
- difficulty concentrating
- difficulties getting to sleep, and having bad dreams
- big feelings in their body, such as: upset tummy, fast heartbeat, tense muscles or feeling numb.

These reactions might settle down naturally with time. As we said, they are **normal responses to difficult experiences**.

So, we've done a lot of work in this chapter. Let's do a safety anchor from Chapter 1 before continuing. Choose one, and make sure someone practises it with you.

Asking the right question: 'What happened to you?'

If we want to understand people well, we must move the focus from asking 'What's wrong with you?' to asking 'What's happened to you?' Language and how we talk about things are important. For example, 'What's wrong with you?' could feel blaming (even if that's not intentional), like there is something wrong with the person; whereas 'What's happened to you?' allows people to understand each other better and develop more empathy for why someone might feel and behave the way they do.

Thinking in this way can help to create a safe environment. Safe environments are important in overcoming the effects of traumatic experiences.

Let's take an example of considering the question 'What's happened to you?':

Callum (15) came to see a psychologist. He asked if he could be diagnosed with ADHD (Attention Deficit Hyperactivity Disorder) because he was struggling to concentrate in class and his teachers were getting cross. The psychologist asked him when his struggles with concentrating started, so Callum shared that it was about a year ago, when Mum got a new boyfriend. The psychologist and Callum met a few times, and eventually he felt safe enough to share that all he could think about at school was whether his mum was safe at home.

He explained that Mum and her boyfriend often argued, and it sometimes got physical. Callum felt he needed to be at home to protect his mum.

The psychologist explained that she didn't think there was anything 'wrong' with him. Of course he was thinking about his mum, and this was impacting his ability to concentrate on other things. The psychologist tried to help by speaking to the adults in his life so they could understand how worried he was. When the school understood, they found a space Callum could go to when he was worried about his mum, and his mum was offered support to help with her safety.

After this, Callum didn't feel the diagnosis of ADHD was right for him, as people around him were more understanding about why it was sometimes hard to concentrate and they had agreed on what the adults could do to support him.

Post-traumatic growth

People can experience positive change after a traumatic experience (but there's no pressure to have a positive change, it's just what some people notice!). This might be a changed perspective, really valuing people who are caring or knowing just how strong you are.

Remember what we said in the previous chapter about surviving and thriving? You might have developed many qualities to cope with your toughest days.

Summary

So, that was a quick whistle-stop tour through what trauma means, experiences that could cause trauma symptoms to develop and the importance of understanding someone's life experiences when looking at how they appear on the surface.

We hope this chapter has helped you understand a bit more about trauma. The following chapters aim to support you in any areas that trauma may be affecting you.

Work through these chapters bit by bit, in your own time and at your own pace, and remember to have compassion for yourself on days you are not feeling OK.

CHAPTER 5

Stories About Yourself

I've learnt that I'm not perfect, no one is, but I'm as good as anyone else. **Carla, 15**

Stories about ourselves

You'll hear descriptions of yourself as you grow up – about what sort of person you were or are now. These stories shape how you might think and feel about yourself. This is called **self-esteem**.

You can think of self-esteem as being a bit like a story – it's the story you have about yourself. It might be based on the tale life tells you about yourself, and it might be positive or negative.

You might have heard stories that say you are bright, funny, caring and kind, good at sports and hardworking. Or you might have heard quite different stories.

The stories you hold about yourself can change over time, like in a book or movie series that has sequels 1, 2 and 3. You can make new stories with new people, learn to rewrite your story and make new chapters in the book of your life.

★ Use the space below to think about the stories you have about yourself. You might hold different stories about yourself at the same time.

1. ....
....

2. ....
....

3. ....
....

Self-esteem is partly just stories you hold about yourself, and for many people, this starts in their early relationships.

If someone has been shown they are likeable and loveable, they might feel these things about themselves as they grow up. They might be confident learning new things, meeting new people and taking on new roles.

If someone has mostly experienced kindness and safety, they learn:

The world: is safe, good things happen

Other people are: mostly kind and caring

I am: likeable (because people are nice to me) and loveable

These beliefs will give them confidence to try new things and meet new people.

But if they grew up with lots of criticism, or with someone who was angry with them a lot, they might learn things like:

The world is: unsafe, often bad things happen

Other people are: unkind, mean to me, hurtful

I am: not likeable (because other people don't treat me like they like me), not nice, bad

For someone with the second set of thoughts, doing new things might be frightening and worrying. They might go into new situations expecting people to be unkind, unfriendly or hurtful. This might mean they hold back more, don't share as much about themselves and find it hard to trust people.

The beliefs you hold about yourself can change the way you think and feel with new people and in new situations.

★   Have a go at finishing the sentences below about your thoughts about yourself, the world and others. You might find these views change over time.

The world is: . . . .

Other people are: . . . .

I am: . . . .

Now take some time to chat about your answers with one of your team to see if they have the same or different views – and why!

What helps?

Right, so we know no one is all good or all bad, but if you've come to think of yourself as bad and want to change it, here's what you can do...

- Challenge negative thoughts. Ask yourself 'Is it really true that I am not kind? What about when I looked after the neighbour's dog? Helped my friend? Looked after my brother?'
- Avoid aiming for perfection – no one is perfect. We all make mistakes and get things wrong sometimes, so don't judge mistakes too harshly. Think about what you might say to your best friend if they made a mistake and try to be a best friend to yourself.
- Look after your body. Get enough sleep and eat well. It's easier to stop bullying thoughts creeping in when you feel healthier.
- Look after your emotional health. Be friends with people who are mostly kind to you.
- Do things that give you a feeling of achievement. This could be in sport, music, volunteering, reading, drawing, art, anything really!
- Remember, often your biggest critic is yourself. Turn down the record on bullying thoughts or change the track in your mind.
- Hold on to positives. Keep a jar in your room and when you do something well, or get a compliment, write it down and put it in the jar. It can be small, like 'I was kind to my friend today' or 'My teacher said I listened well.' You'll soon see them mount up; then, when you are having a bad day, look in the jar.
- Make yourself a 'compassion pebble' as a reminder to be kind to yourself (see Chapter 6).
- Rewrite your story about yourself based on new relationships and experiences.
- Remember, we all have lots of different strengths and qualities. It's OK to have different qualities to your friends. These differences make you *you*! Look at the next page, which lists lots of qualities you might have.
- Remember, we are all a mix of different qualities – no one is all good or all bad.

★ POSITIVE QUALITIES THAT I SHOW OR AM DEVELOPING

Highlight or circle the qualities you show or are developing below and add any more that you can think of.

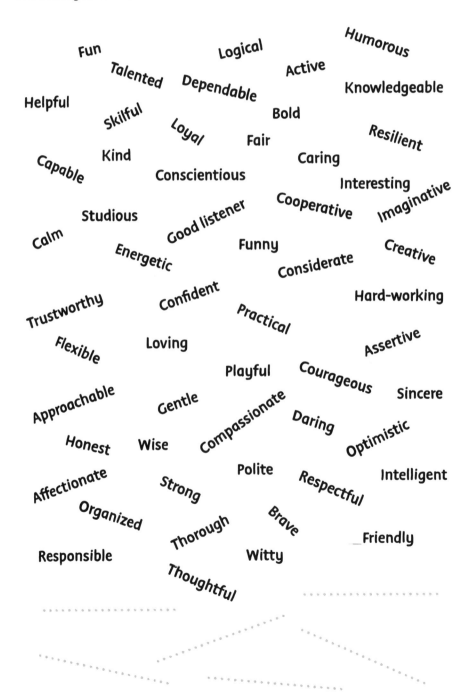

Fun
Logical
Humorous
Talented Dependable Active
Knowledgeable
Helpful
Skilful Loyal Bold
Fair Resilient
Capable Kind Caring
Conscientious Interesting
Studious Cooperative Imaginative
Calm Good listener Funny Creative
Energetic Considerate
Trustworthy Confident Hard-working
Practical
Flexible Loving Assertive
Playful Courageous
Approachable Gentle Sincere
Compassionate Daring Optimistic
Honest Wise
Polite Intelligent
Affectionate Strong Respectful
Organized Brave
Thorough _Friendly
Responsible Witty
Thoughtful

CHAPTER 6

Compassion

Another skill to practise is kindness – to yourself.

It's important to be compassionate to others, but first you'll need to learn to be compassionate to yourself. This includes noticing when bullying thoughts are talking to you negatively. Remind yourself that:

- no one is perfect
- it is OK to be imperfect
- it's OK to feel your emotions
- it's OK to not be OK all the time.

Notice negative statements like 'I'm bad' or 'I'm an idiot', and let go of these or challenge them. Write them down, and then decide what you want to do with them. You might want to rip or screw up the paper or throw it away to remind yourself that you don't have to accept bullying thoughts.

It might be hard at first, but compassion is like a plant – if you water it daily with practice, it will begin to grow. Knowing you are a 'good-enough person' as you are creates a strong foundation for life.

Take a break: pebbles

Mindfulness pebbles

We talked about grounding in the present environment. A great way to do this is to practise 'mindfulness' with an object. Mindfulness sounds complicated, but it's actually super simple – let's try.

Pick up a pebble that you like. You might like its colour, shape or feel. If you can't find a pebble, find another object that is satisfying to hold.

1. Hold it in your hand.
2. Sit straight and relaxed, breathing in.
3. Feel the weight of the pebble in your hand – is it heavy or light?
4. What is the texture? Is it rough, smooth, jagged?
5. What does it look like? Is the surface shiny or dull?
6. Is it one colour or a mix of colours?
7. Is it large or small?
8. How does it feel in your hand?
9. While you are doing this, you don't need to think about the future or the past, just the present moment.

When you really focused on the pebble, did you notice that you were in the moment, not thinking about anything other than the pebble?

This is the essence of 'mindfulness' – it's when we are mindful of our surroundings and focused on the present moment.

Compassion pebbles

Turn your favourite pebbles into reminders of messages you want to focus on – it's fun to do, especially with other people!

Decorate the pebbles with pictures that mean something to you or words you want to remember. Use gel pens and seal the pattern with glue or varnish to give a glossy finish and make them waterproof.

You can get these out whenever you need them.

Compassion-focused approach

There is a whole theory about compassion and how important it is to wellbeing.

Basically, it says people have three systems: the threat, drive and soothing systems. Ideally, we want our soothing system to kick in quickly when we need it, so we can calm ourselves or allow ourselves to be soothed by other people if we need to relax. If the soothing system is slow to get going, or not easy to access, it can be hard to get ourselves calm again. The threat system keeps us alert to dangers (e.g., angry faces or bullying) and the drive system gets us motivated (like getting up for college or working towards an exam).

Problems can occur if we get stuck in one system for more time than is helpful. For example, when a threat has gone but we're still stuck in the threat system. For example, if you had been bullied, you still might not feel safe to go to the dinner hall even after the bullying stopped. Being stuck in the threat system would stop you eating your lunch with your other friends, even once the bullying had ended.

Sometimes we might find it hard to turn on the soothing system when we need it (meaning we can't relax or feel comforted easily).

Problems can also happen if our system is not balanced, so if the threat system is much bigger than the compassion system, you might notice feeling under stress often and not feeling able to soothe yourself. Equally, if the drive system is out of balance and too strong, you might notice that you are over-revising for exams and unable to take rest when needed.

The example below shows a threat system that is out of balance with the soothe and drive systems, which could leave the person feeling anxious, stressed and unable to relax.

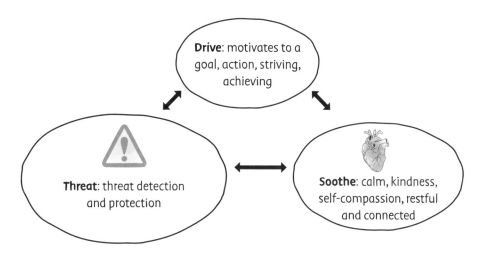

In this example, the aim would be to get the systems back in balance by reducing feelings of threat, increasing feelings of safety and finding ways to activate the soothing system. When in the soothing system, someone would feel relaxed and able to connect with other people. This idea is called Compassion-Focused Therapy (CFT).

Remember!
It's useful to know when you're in each system and how to move between them. It's particularly useful to learn how to get your soothing system going when you want to chillax.

To help activate the soothing system, focus on:

encouragement balance
relaxing connection
wellbeing restore pets
movement warmth acceptance music safety
rest contentment repair compassion
support kindness calmness walking

★ MY COMPASSION PAGE

The important things to work out are:

What system do I spend a lot of time in?

....
....

My threat system is mostly activated when/where/with:

....
....
....

My drive system is mostly activated when/where/with:

....
....
....

My compassion or soothing system is mostly activated when/where/with:

....
....
....

Things that I find soothing:

....
....
....

Other people could help me access my soothing system by:

....
....
....

CHAPTER 7

Sleep

Bedtimes used to be tough. I'd find it hard to keep the bad memories away at night, they'd keep going round my mind, and in the dark with no distractions it was hard. I still find it tough sometimes, but I have realized I sleep better if I've taken Buddy [dog] for a walk. It helps me feel tired, so I get to sleep quicker. **Sunny, 17**

You might have heard adults complaining that teenagers sleep ALL the time. In fact, teenagers do need more sleep than adults. The teenage brain is growing and changing, so sleep is important.

Sleep can be amazing. Sleep is really good for your health, mood, brain functioning and wellbeing.

If you wake up feeling great after eight hours, you can probably skip this section. But for lots of people, getting good sleep can be hard.

Random, interesting sleep fact: 12% of people dream completely in black and white.

When sleep is not your friend

It's hard to be awake in the middle of the night counting down the hours until you have to be up again. Sleep is affected by diet, stress and exercise – so what can you do if you are struggling to sleep?

Exercise

Exercise is great at helping to get a good night's sleep. This could be walking, jogging, cycling, football, going to the gym – anything that gets you moving. Burning off adrenaline during the day and wearing out muscles really helps with sleep.

Routine

A relaxing routine before bed isn't just for kids! As teens, or adults, we also need a good routine at night. This sends signals to your brain that say 'Now's the time to get sleepy!' Doing the same thing each evening before bed helps your brain to learn 'This is the time to settle and switch off for sleep.'

Like all animals, we need to feel safe before we can fall asleep. Having a calm routine creates a feeling of safety, as it tells our brains there is nothing different to worry about or pay attention to.

Screen-free time

Blue light from screens keeps the brain active, making it harder to sleep, so reading a magazine, book or anything that does not emit light before bed is better than reading from a phone.

Racing thoughts or emotions

It's hard to sleep if you've got loads on your mind! It might be worries about the next day or upsetting memories from the past.

Try keeping a notepad and pen by your bed to get the thoughts out of your mind and onto the paper.

You could try asking yourself 'Is this something that I can do anything about now?' If it's not:

- watch the thought float away on a cloud
- place the thought on a leaf and let it drift down a river in your mind.

Nightmares or bad dreams

When something scary or threatening has happened, our brain tries to make sense of it. A lot of this happens during sleep and in dreams.

If something scary happened to you and you are having bad dreams, it might be a sign your brain is working hard to process it. This is useful in the long term, but it can be frightening and upsetting.

If your nightmare relates to something scary that happened to you, you might be able to do something in the daytime to help you sleep. When something frightening has happened, you might try not to think about it – to avoid feeling sad, upset or scared. But if you avoid thinking about it during the day, it's more likely to pop up during sleep, causing nightmares.

If you feel able to, try to process this experience gradually during the daytime. You can process an experience by talking to someone, writing, drawing or painting about the thing that happened. Make sure you do this in a way that feels safe, when you are ready and with someone you trust.

Another technique some people use is to try and take control of their bad dream and do a bit of 'nightmare rescripting' when they're awake. To do this, it's helpful to enlist the support of someone in your trusted team. Speak or think through what happened in your bad dream, but this time say what would have to happen in the dream for you to end up in a safe place. Who would you bring into the dream to help or support you? How would you get out of the situation and into a safer and calmer place?

Remember!

- What we do during the day influences how well we sleep at night.
- If sleep is not your friend, exercise, a good diet, routine and looking after your emotional wellbeing will help.
- Nightmares can be scary, but they can be your brain's way of making sense of things that have happened.

Use the chart on the next page to keep track of your sleep across the week. It might show how things like exercise, caffeine, screen time and routines impact your sleep. Be kind to yourself – changing your sleep pattern takes time, as you are retraining your brain about when to feel sleepy.

★ SLEEP CHART

Day	Hours of sleep	Exercise	Caffeine	Routine	Screens
Monday	....	☐	☐	☐	☐
Tuesday	....	☐	☐	☐	☐
Wednesday	....	☐	☐	☐	☐
Thursday	....	☐	☐	☐	☐
Friday	....	☐	☐	☐	☐
Saturday	....	☐	☐	☐	☐
Sunday	....	☐	☐	☐	☐

★ ALL ABOUT MY SLEEP

On a scale of 1–5, my sleep is generally (1 = not good, 5 = great!):

1	2	3	4	5
Not good				Great

I sleep best when:

....

....

....

....

What gets in the way of my sleep is:

....

....

....

....

Who can help with making the evening more relaxing?

....

....

....

....

One thing that might help my sleep is:

....

....

....

....

....

CHAPTER 8

Eating and Movement

Here's a random food fact: Hawaiian pizza wasn't created in Hawaii or in Italy – it was actually created in Canada!

Pizza distractions aside, this chapter is in the journal because eating and food are really important for emotional wellbeing. Your mind and body are connected, so looking after one looks after the other.

When we don't value ourselves, this can be seen in our eating habits. For example, if you feel like you don't deserve good things, you may not give your body the food it really needs. Healthy foods like vegetables, fish, meat, eggs and fruit contain vitamins and minerals that the body needs to work. If you don't get enough of these, you may get unwell more often and feel more tired.

Diet also affects mood: you might feel more irritable, tired and low without the right vitamins and minerals. Think of your body as a car – cars run on petrol, diesel or electricity. If you put lemonade in the engine, it probably wouldn't go very far...

Sugar gives you an initial buzz, but afterwards it can make you feel more anxious, stressed and tired (although sugar and chocolate are a nice treat sometimes).

Eating good food and eating enough food are both great ways to take care of yourself.

The 'Inner Squirrel'

When I was little my mum and dad would fight a lot. When they were fighting, I didn't want to come out of my room, but sometimes it would go on for ages and I'd get hungry. I started taking food out of the fridge and keeping it under my bed so I had it for later if I needed it.
Kendall, 13

Food is really important to survival. You need food every day, and you need enough of it to give your body the energy and nutrition it needs. Sometimes, children find that there is not enough food when they are growing up. It might be that the adult:

- doesn't shop regularly
- doesn't make regular meals
- doesn't always have enough money for food.

Some people who've grown up without enough food learn to keep safe by saving food to be eaten later. If other food runs out, they've got some stored to rely on. Food might also be kept in a bedroom if it doesn't always feel safe to go to the kitchen.

If there are often arguments between adults in a child's home, hiding food upstairs may be a survival strategy to avoid confrontation, as Kendall explained.

Changing eating habits

If you are used to not having enough food and then your situation changes and you are living somewhere with enough food, it may take your brain and behaviour time to catch up.

Because food is necessary for survival, the urge to store food can feel very powerful. In a new situation, it might take time to realize that storing food isn't needed any more.

Have you ever watched a squirrel in the autumn? They bury nuts in lots of places ready for the winter when there will be less food around. If you reliably give squirrels lots of nuts every day, they will still carry on burying them, just in case.

If you know this is something you do, ask yourself: 'What will help your inner squirrel to relax, so you don't need to keep burying nuts?'

If you have been in this situation and find yourself storing food when you don't need to, don't get mad at your brain – it's just doing its job and looking out for you! But it might be confusing for your parent or carer if they don't know this and keep finding lots of food wrappers under the bed.

Some people notice they overeat when food is available. There might have been times when it was helpful to eat as much as possible when there was food.

If you notice yourself taking food to your room to store for later, ask yourself 'Do I still need to do this?', 'Is this something that is still helpful to me?'

Undereating

Sometimes, when people are feeling low or not good enough, they don't eat enough. They might restrict their food as a way of not letting themselves have nice things or be overly focused on being a certain size or shape. If this is the case for you, it might be that you are overvaluing weight and shape (and undervaluing yourself!).

Think about the friend or family member you like most in the world and then think about why you picked them. Make a pie like the one below to include all the things you like about them and how important each quality is; it could look something like:

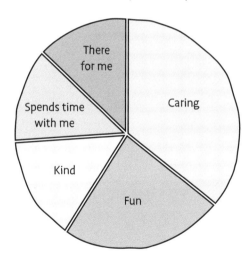

Qualities I like in my favourite person

You will notice that the way the person looks and their weight are not why you love or like them. And it's the same the other way round! So, if in your mind, what you imagine is important about you is...

What I think people value about me

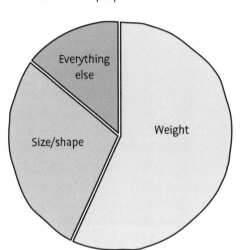

...this is missing so many of your qualities! Focus on all the qualities people like and love about you and remember: weight, shape and size are not important in our reasons for liking people. Also, remember that bodies do so much for us – they are not just our external appearance. They need to perform so many functions for us every day, so make sure you allow yourself the food you need to thrive!

Movement
Movement is a great way of keeping well. It also helps calm our moods. Calming the body with movement makes it harder for fight, flight and freeze (more on this in Chapter 10) to get activated.

Remember!
Looking after our bodies really helps with looking after our minds. Getting enough good food, sleep and exercise are important foundations for our mood. If these three things are going well, it can reduce anxiety and improve mood. So:

Good eating = healthy body = healthy mind = healthy moods!

★ CREATING MOVEMENT

Some ways to create movement are given below. Circle those you enjoy or might want to try.

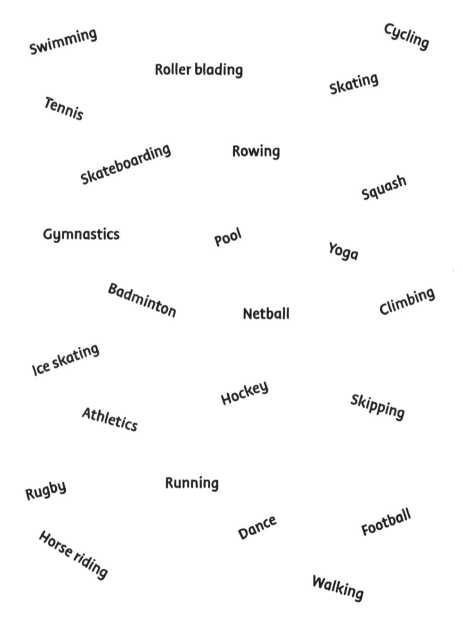

Swimming

Cycling

Roller blading

Skating

Tennis

Skateboarding

Rowing

Squash

Gymnastics

Pool

Yoga

Badminton

Netball

Climbing

Ice skating

Hockey

Skipping

Athletics

Rugby

Running

Horse riding

Dance

Football

Walking

CHAPTER 9

Attachments and Why They Are Important

What attachment means and why it matters

You may or may not have heard people talk about 'attachment'. This chapter is about why we all make attachments and what this means.

Picture a baby, brand new in the world. Let's pretend baby can think clear thoughts and that we can hear them. Let's tune in...

'I can't hold up my own head, I need milk, I need warmth, I need to be protected, my nappy needs changing, I need love...how do I get all these things?... CRY!'

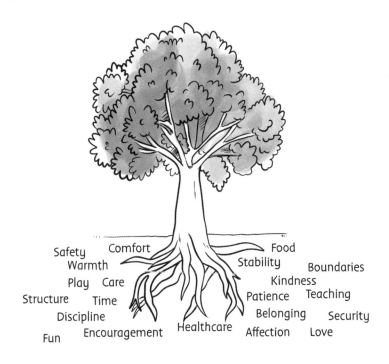

Safety Comfort Food
Warmth Stability Boundaries
Play Care Kindness
Structure Time Patience Teaching
Discipline Belonging Security
Fun Encouragement Healthcare Affection Love

So, our baby can't do anything for himself. He needs someone to look after him, give him food, love and warmth and keep him safe. Hopefully, baby's parent sees or hears these cries and takes care of him, providing lots of the things he needs.

Some of what children need is shown in the roots of the tree. When parents provide this enough of the time, babies and children have a strong, safe foundation from which they can grow.

First, emotions

Have you noticed that babies have very strong emotions? They are either laughing or crying like it's the end of the world!

So back to our baby: when mum or dad comes to him, they give him what he needs, and he calms down. He thinks 'I've got my milk now, I'm nice and warm, I'm being cuddled, all is OK again'.

Our baby learns over time that parents work out what is wrong, they fix it and he feels better. The parent will also communicate that they know what the baby needs, helping give language for their internal experience. Saying 'You must be hungry' will connect the feeling in his tummy with the word 'hunger' – over time, this helps baby have words for feelings in his body. Baby is learning that adults help and can be trusted to get things right and that upsetting emotions don't last forever. If he could think in clear thoughts, we might hear 'When I cry, someone comes to help me and I usually feel better.' They would learn that:

Adults = good and helpful
Emotions = I get upset but I feel better again soon
Baby (self) = people care about me and help me

Baby is learning; big emotions pass, discomfort gets better and adults are helpful. Later in life, he might take this learning into other places, like school, expecting adults to be kind, caring and helpful.

Our baby is learning 'If I ask for something, I get the help I need'

Remember!
All babies need to keep a big person close, because they can't do anything for themselves, like get food or keep themselves safe. This means they really need to bond with an adult to keep the adult close to them.

This means attachment is really important for survival! But know that, often, things can be different to the picture above; let's think together about how.

'Listen to me!' baby

Babies and young children learn patterns for the best way to keep their parent close and get what they need, like milk, food or cuddles.

Usually when I do this, Mum does that

Sometimes, babies and young children learn that if they cry long or loud enough, mum or dad will come eventually.

Let's picture our baby again. This time he's in a different home, having a different experience. Sometimes his mum and dad come to him when he cries, and sometimes they don't. He starts to notice that if he cries louder and louder for long enough, mum or dad come in the end. Brilliant! He has found a way to get his milk, nappy changed and cuddles: 'Just cry LOUDER and LOUDER and get more and more upset until they come!'

Over time, baby learns this pattern for getting his parents' care, and it becomes a habit (which makes sense – he's just worked out the best way to get what he needs). He watches his parents closely to check if they are noticing what he needs.

'Keeping quiet' baby

OK, so now back to baby, but in a third house. This parent is the opposite of our last parent. Rather than come to the baby if he cries louder, this parent is more likely to come when baby is quiet.

This parent finds it hard to stay close to baby when he is crying. Crying louder doesn't work well for getting his parents to come and do the things he needs – they are more likely to go away when he cries.

My mum leaves the room when I cry

If our baby had clear thoughts, he might think 'I need milk, I need warmth, how best to get these things? I'll try not to cry so I can keep them near.' OK, he doesn't think this, but he starts to make the connection that if he's crying, his mum or dad leave the room and if he's quiet, they come back. This doesn't mean he doesn't need anything; it just means he's noticed that he gets these things quicker if he doesn't cry. So, this is the opposite of baby in our second house.

As he needs to stay close to a parent to survive, he learns that the best way to keep them close is to not cry or show when he is upset.

So, baby is really clever. Whatever home he is in, he adapts to his carers! He learns to keep them close – either by crying more or crying less – to make sure they take care of him.

When parents find it hard to respond to their baby

Lastly, let's think about our baby in a fourth home. This one is most difficult to think about and is best read through with your team.

This time, when baby is hungry, is cold or needs his nappy changing, he cries, but when he does, Mum or Dad might: shout at him, get very upset themselves or even hurt him. In this house, when he cries or shows he needs his parent, they respond in a way that frightens him. If baby had clear thoughts, he might say:

> I need milk, warmth and my nappy changed, but when I cry, I get shouted at. I don't know what to do. I need someone to take care of me, but when I ask it's scary and I don't know what to expect.

If this happens often and over a long time, this is confusing for him, because the person he needs to help him is also the person that scares him.

His parent may respond differently on different days – sometimes positively, with hugs, warmth and food, and other times angrily – shouting, hitting out or crying. This would make it hard for him to know the best way to approach his parents.

He wants his parent near (because he needs them) but is also scared of them, so he might withdraw when a parent is nearby.

Parents might respond this way if they have problems with alcohol or illegal drugs or because they have their own difficulties that get in the way of them noticing these signs.

There is space on the next page to think about how your first caregiver might have responded to you. Remember, if you want to, you can involve someone you trust when completing this.

★ MY EARLY EXPERIENCES

What might my parent/carer have done most when I cried?

What makes me think this?

I think I used to try to get my needs met by:

Which of the patterns might best fit with what things were like for me?

You might struggle to remember what things were like for you when you were younger. Don't worry if that's the case; it can be helpful to think more generally about how you feel when you get upset in the here and now – how do you let out your 'cry for help?' Do you cry (show your distress) quite loudly? Do you bottle your cry (distress) up and not let people see how you feel? Do you feel unsure about what to do with your distress and feel very confused and overwhelmed?

Whilst we're thinking about baby times and what we need when we are young, it's helpful to think about how we need adults to help us learn about feelings and emotions. When we're young, we need adults to help us recognize and have the language to express our feelings, as well as to learn how to cope with emotions. We aren't born knowing what hunger, sadness and tiredness mean or feel like! If we have adults that can 'tune in' to our feelings and help us understand and have words for them, this really helps us to recognize when we're sad, hungry or tired ourselves as we get older. We can then tell others we need help or even soothe the emotions ourselves when we're older. If people haven't had this from others, they might struggle to understand or name day-to-day emotions.

What's it like for you? How do you know when you're sad, angry, hungry or tired and how did you learn what these feelings are?

Remember!
Everyone has an attachment style, but they grow and change as we connect with new people. So, it's just helpful to understand your style and where it came from and to think about where you want it to go from here.

- Everyone has an attachment pattern.
- It's not a science; it's just about patterns that people some-times show.
- Attachment patterns are between people, not within one person.
- Attachment patterns can change over time – they are not fixed.
- Attachment patterns describe a way of being in relationships with other people.
- These are not 'facts' but are ideas about how people relate to each other. If they are helpful to you then use them; if not, ignore them.

- No parents are perfect; it's about being 'good enough'.

Adverse community environments

Remember we talked about adverse childhood experiences in Chapter 4? Well, people also talk about adverse community environments. These are things in the community that might make a situation more stressful for a family and are outside of the parent's control. This could include: racism, discrimination, poverty and housing issues. This wider context around a family is important, as these things can put extra pressure on a family unfairly. For example, economic hardship, like difficulty finding work or high cost of housing, can mean it is difficult to buy all the resources a family needs or can mean that parents are working long hours to support a family. These external factors are important and unfairly disadvantage some people more than others. So let's just remember that we all live in a wider context as we continue to think about parenting.

Parents are people too

Let's think about parents more.

Sometimes, people find it hard to do all the things that babies and toddlers need. Remember we said above that there might be wider things that are making this tough, like financial issues, employment or other pressures.

A parent might find it hard to do practical things, like:

- buying and cooking food
- paying bills for electricity
- taking their child to the doctor or dentist.

Or they might also be finding it hard to do emotional things, like:

- listening to their child when they are upset, cuddling them when they cry or helping them when they've had a scary dream
- finding time for fun things like play, which helps them learn.

Often, parents want to do these things well, but something gets in the way of this, meaning they find being a parent hard. For example, if a parent had to work two jobs, they might feel very tired and not have enough energy to enjoy fun time together.

We've briefly thought about some of the important wider factors; let's think of some of other possible reasons a parent might find it hard to give their baby everything they need.

They didn't have those things done for them when they were growing up

They might have missed out on these things in their own childhood and not be sure how to do them for their own child. If they didn't have enough love and care when they were young, or had a parent who scared them, they might not know what to do when they have their own child. Some parents end up doing the same things that their parent did to them, even without meaning to.

Their own stuff!

Some parents have big emotions of their own that they find hard to manage. That's not your fault or your job to manage, but it's useful to be aware of so you know what is your stuff and what is their stuff! They might be feeling very sad, anxious or scared themselves, which might get in the way of doing the practical and emotional things their child needs. All parents will feel this sometimes, but for some, big feelings are around very often or feel very hard to manage.

Illegal drugs or too much alcohol

Some parents have problems with too much alcohol or illegal drugs. If this is a problem, it can make parenting harder. It might mean they: spend a lot of money on this and don't have money for food, do not always respond, are tired often or are very changeable in mood. When someone becomes 'addicted' to drugs or alcohol, this can have a really big impact on their minds and bodies: they find it very hard to stop using them even if they know the negative consequences. This can be really frustrating and worrying if this is an adult you care about.

> Having one of these problems doesn't always impact parenting. Someone might struggle with one of these but still be able to do the practical and emotional things needed very well. How people parent is a mix of: things that happened to them, their resources, external pressures, how they feel and how much support they have.

How it might feel for you

You might have a mix of feelings if any of these problems have been around. It is OK to have two or more different feelings about someone or something at the same time. For example, some young people say they care about their parents but find it too upsetting to be around them. Some young people might say they really want to see a family member but cannot for some reason, and they may have strong feelings about that too. All situations are different, so if any of this is happening, remember to talk it through with your trusted adult as often as you need to.

Having strong conflicting emotions about the same person can feel confusing. Remember that all your feelings are valid, even if they seem to clash in some way.

Remember!

None of these things happened because of anything you did. The things you've read that shape parents might be things that you care about a lot, but they are also things you probably won't have any influence over. If this is taking a lot of your energy, try to put that into things you **can** control in your own life. You probably won't be able to completely stop thinking about things you can't control, but try to push energy into things you can control (the other things will still be there, but not taking up all your focus!).

Who doesn't love a metaphor?

Let's imagine we are standing right in front of a tree. If you stand really close to it so it is next to your eyes, the tree will be the only thing you can see (go and try!). If you then move back a little, you can still see the tree, but you can also see the grass, a sheep in the field and the sky. The tree hasn't gone away – it's still there, but it's no longer taking up the whole view. Life can be like this – if we really focus on one thing, it can get in the way of seeing other things around us. So, we can practise keeping the tree in mind and taking in the rest of the view.

The rest of the view might be spending energy on friends, school work, days out, ice skating, football, time with other family or carers, or many other things!

★ DEBRIEF SO FAR

As you go through this journal, it might give you lots to think about. There is some space below to summarize your thoughts, topics that brought up big feelings, things you want to talk through and new things to try.

Summary of ideas so far:	Topics that brought up strong feelings:
Things I'd like to talk about with an important adult:	**New things to try:**

CHAPTER 10

Fight, Flight and Freeze (3 F)

Have you noticed that when you feel scared, your body does lots of strange things? In this chapter we'll look at what happens when we feel scared. This is called our fight, flight and freeze response.

When we feel under threat, our body releases stress hormones. These tell our muscles: there is something to be scared about – so get ready!

Let's imagine...

There you are one night, watching TV. The living room door opens and in walks a MASSIVE TIGER!

Eyes say 'WHAT, open wide, watch out, watch out!'

Brain says 'Ahhh, alarm, alarm, send out the stress hormones, NOW!'

Heart says 'Wow, loads of stress hormones (Brain must know something bad is happening), send beats per minute to MAX!'

Stomach says 'Tighten up, no time for eating, time not to GET eaten!'

Muscles say 'Legs and arms ready, hit tiger on the head or get running out the door!'

Bladder or gut might say 'Release liquids/solids now (need to go to the toilet), we need to get rid of this extra weight so we're lighter to run away!'

OK, so these days, it's not going to be a tiger in our living room, but sometimes it really feels like our body doesn't know that!

Our body and brain treat lots of different things in the world as a 'threat' in the same way. In modern life, this huge body response could be caused by: a person being threatening, someone shouting or even interviews and exams.

We might get that same bodily process – heart racing, rapid breathing, wide eyes, lots of blood flow to our arms and legs and all the blood draining from our stomach – in a maths exam!

It's a super-clever body response designed to keep you safe if you bump into that tiger, but when your body alarm is set off when you don't want it, it can be really annoying!

When this happens, your brain works differently too. Some parts of your brain become very active (the parts that notice fear), and other parts become less active (the bits that do your English homework!). This makes sense, because you wouldn't want to have a long conversation with the tiger; you'd want to get out of there!

Tigers, zebras and watering holes

Whilst we're thinking about our reaction to tigers, it's helpful to take a minute to think about the human brain and how it is different to a zebra's brain (this will make sense, I promise!).

Imagine a zebra in the African desert. This zebra is having a drink out of a watering hole when suddenly a tiger appears! The zebra's brain will (probably) trigger a flight response and rightly so! The zebra will run away to get to safety. Imagine a human in this exact same situation: the human is having a drink from the watering hole, a tiger comes over and, in the same way, the human's brain will trigger a fight, flight or freeze response to run away or maybe stay completely still so the tiger doesn't see them.

Now let's imagine both the zebra and human survive and get away to safety (phew). The difference between the zebra and the human is that the next day, the zebra goes back to the same watering hole for a drink, forgetting what happened the day before. Whereas if the human were asked to go back, they would likely say 'HELL NO! No way am I EVER going back to that watering hole, or any other watering hole again!' In this situation, we would agree with this human – it's probably best to avoid watering holes frequented by wild tigers! The human learns from one experience and applies it to other similar situations.

Sometimes, though, when the 'danger' happens within a relationship, you can see tigers (danger) in other relationships and situations when they might not be there. We can become too cautious and frightened to connect with people. A helpful question to ask might be 'Where do I see and react to tigers? Are the tigers really there?'

Use the space on the following page to draw or write what situations set off this reaction in your body.

★ WHAT ARE MY TRIGGERS OR 'TIGERS'?

Draw or write what sets off your stress response:

The science

When we are in what we see as a threatening situation, we get a big response in our body:

- our heart beats faster to push blood around our body
- our breathing quickens to get more oxygen to muscles
- muscles tense ready for action.

★ You can use the drawing below to note down what happens in your body when you feel under stress.

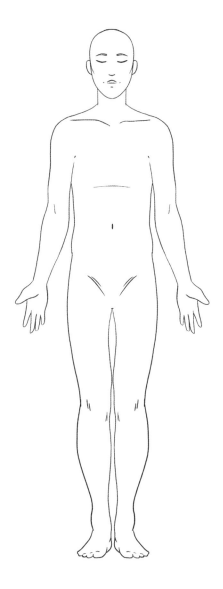

Fight, flight and freeze

With all that energy in your body, it's no wonder there can be some big reactions!

Fight: One reaction is to want to fight back. This is helpful in a situation where you are in physical danger. Your body gets a big burst of energy ready to get your muscles working.

Flight: You might find you want to run off. When stress hormones are released, you get lots of energy in your muscles, like your leg muscles. Flight can be your body's way of protecting you by getting you out of the situation. If your flight response gets triggered, you might run off during an argument.

Freeze: When animals are in a dangerous situation they can't escape, they sometimes 'freeze' or 'play dead'. This can be a way of trying not to be noticed. In freeze, people feel the same amount of fear, which generates the same energy as fight, but they are unable to release the energy by fighting or fleeing. In freeze, the person can't follow the impulse to move and therefore can't let go of this energy.

Some people describe not feeling present when they are in freeze. This can be a way of distancing from upsetting emotions (such as fear) or unpleasant physical feelings in the body (like pain) when running away is not possible.

★   You can use the space below to note down whether the fight, flight and freeze responses happen to you and in what situations.

Response	Happens to me?	Situation(s)
Fight	☐	....
		....
		....
Flight	☐	....
		....
		....
Freeze	☐	....
		....
		....

Over-triggered alarms

Have you ever seen a car where the alarm is going off all the time? You just have to get close and the alarm starts sounding. Well, sometimes our stress response can become too easily triggered, like that car alarm, and we find it's going off when we don't want it to! So fight, flight and freeze might get triggered when it's not helpful. This overactive alarm usually happens if someone has been through lots of stressful situations in the past.

Summary

When it's under high stress, the body releases stress hormones, which cause:

- fight
- flight
- freeze.

These can be useful in a dangerous situation but can become over-learned and easily triggered in situations where they are unhelpful. An example is if you were told off by your teacher and this produced a fight response! It wouldn't solve the problem and would probably make things worse!

If your fight, flight and freeze response is triggered, it might be a sign you are finding the situation overwhelming or that it triggered a memory from the past.

Below are some situations where fight and flight might be helpful and times when fight, flight and freeze might be unhelpful.

Situations where fight and flight are helpful

- Being attacked.
- Being chased.
- In physical danger.

Situations where fight, flight and freeze are unhelpful

- Disagreement with teacher.
- Verbal argument with friend.
- Exam/job interview.

★ MY 3 F RESPONSES: FIGHT, FLIGHT AND FREEZE

Under stress, I think my body usually reacts with 3 F responses:

- ☐ Fight
- ☐ Fiight
- ☐ Freeze

I think this, because at times of stress I notice:

....

....

....

....

When fight, flight and freeze happens, I tend to:

....

....

....

....

When I am in fight, flight and freeze, what really helps me to calm is:

....

....

....

....

When this happens, what I would like from other people is:

....

....

....

....

What helps?

Fight, flight and freeze use a lot of energy, so it's very tiring! The good news is that big stress responses don't last more than 60–90 minutes. The body uses up the stress hormones in that time and you go back to how you felt before. **That means that when this big feeling is happening, you can remind yourself that it won't last forever.**

★ Write yourself coping statements, for example, 'I've felt this way before but I know it passes', 'I won't feel this stressed for much longer.'

....

....

....

....

....

....

3 F in overdrive!

Stress hormones release energy into the body in a short burst. Sometimes though, if people have experienced lots of stress in their life, they can find that fight, flight and freeze are easily triggered (because they are a well-worn pathway in the brain).

> *I was so stressed by everything that'd happened, like mum's drinking, moving to my dad's and worrying about my brothers, that I was kind of full. Any little thing would push me over the edge and I'd end up exploding. My support worker has been helping me learn how to empty my 'stress bucket' a bit at a time so it doesn't spill over as often.* **Tommy, 17**

If you think of fight, flight and freeze as being like a speedometer on a car, people whose early life was calm might be cruising mostly at 30 mph. When something stressful happens, their speedo temporarily goes up to 70 mph, but when the stressor has gone (or after a bit of time) it goes back down to 30 mph and they're relaxed again.

If someone has grown up in a very stressful environment, the speedometer can:

- accelerate faster
- go up to 70 mph when someone who has not had these experiences might stay cruising
- come back down from 70 mph to 30 mph more slowly.

If there is often shouting, fighting or people getting hurt when you are growing up, your body learns to keep you prepared with more of those stress hormones. This might have been helpful at times – like keeping you alert to unsafe sounds.

If things are now settled, it might not be so helpful. If a new stressor comes along – like a teacher shouting – on top of these existing stress hormones, it might send the speedometer over the limit!

The good news is that because this is a learned pathway, you can also learn something new! You can help your body:

- notice when the speedometer is creeping up and help it to slow down
- learn to calm again when the speedometer has hit 70 mph
- stay relaxed in the longer term, so the speedometer is less likely to reach 70 mph in the first place.

Once you know whether you usually react with fight, flight and freeze, you can explain to someone you trust – at school and at home – why this might happen and what they can do to help.

Our brains

Our brains are totally weird and wonderful, so let's find out more about them. Random interesting brain fact: we are not born with all our brain abilities ready to be used – our brains keep developing into our mid-20s!

You can think of your brain as being like a house with different rooms. Let's look in the rooms to see what's there, starting in the oldest room: the basement...

Basement: Wow, there is a really old lizard in there. Old lizard's been there a really long time. He's good at spotting danger, so he does the 'quick, out of the way or you'll get eaten' stuff. He doesn't really use words. But he's useful. He notices danger, so he would spot that tiger pretty fast. When he spots danger, he presses the panic alarm for the whole body.

He also worries about whether you're warm enough and if you are tired, and he tells your heart how fast to beat. He's in charge of basic survival, so he's pretty important. Let's leave him for now and go up the stairs to the next room...

First floor: It's loud in here! There's a noisy monkey in the first-floor room. Monkey deals with emotions, how we behave and memory.

Sometimes old lizard tells him there is danger and he gets really worked up and loud. Him and old lizard sometimes press the panic alarm and set off that fight, flight and freeze response! When the red button hasn't been pushed, monkey works the levers of the reward systems, so he's quite busy. He keeps us moving forward with things we need to do, like homework or sports. If we meet our goals, he gets a big reward and is really happy.

Penthouse: In here, there's a wise owl on a perch. He sorts out all the most complicated stuff. He weighs up options and makes the big decisions. Wise owl is good at planning, and when lizard and monkey are quiet and calm, he can think clearly and get on with running the show. He likes to do the crossword when he can get lizard and monkey to be quiet for a while! Owl is the newest member of the house – he keeps growing and forming well into our 20s. Whatever our age, though, he sometimes gets shouted down by monkey and lizard in the floors below.

Getting owl back in charge

When we are in fight, flight and freeze, the older parts of our brain (the lizard and the monkey) are running the show. It's hard to think, explain or reason when we are experiencing strong emotions, because lizard and monkey can't do these things. Owl cannot think clearly in fight, flight and freeze. The best way to get owl back in control is to soothe lizard and monkey by letting them know it's safe. They will then let go of the alarm button and owl can get back in charge.

When you next feel worked up about something, notice who is in charge. Is it lizard, monkey or owl?

★ WHO'S IN CHARGE?

Look at each of the statements below and work out who's in charge in each situation. Check your answers at the end of the journal. Write the statements on the grid.

Doing my homework quietly

Shouting at my teacher

Running off after an argument

Choosing a film to watch from a list

Enjoying a chat with my friend

Slamming the car door after a row

Throwing something in my room

Organizing a day out with friends

Owl	Lizard and monkey

Neuroplasticity (brain gym!)

Neuroplasticity sounds like a really complicated word! But it's just the brain's ability to change when things around us change. So, even if lizard or monkey have got used to being in charge, there's no reason why that can't change in the future. We are capable of learning new things all the time.

The brain is about connections – millions of them, a bit like the wires in a computer. Our connections can form patterns, so if we have done something lots of times, the brain forms a well-worn pathway, like a high-speed motorway. The more we practise something, the faster and smoother the connection gets – think back to learning to tie shoelaces or to write your name: the more you practise the more natural it feels, and eventually, you can do it without thinking too much.

The good news is that our brains don't stay the same – they're constantly growing and changing, especially when we are younger. These are the three times when there is the most change:

1. **Early childhood**: Our brains develop a lot in early childhood when they are growing and making new connections.
2. **Teenage years**: They have another intense burst of development in the teenage years (which is why teenagers sleep a lot!).
3. **In our 20s**: They keep changing well into the middle of our 20s, mostly in the areas of the brain that do our most complex thinking and planning.

Learning

Think of all the things we learn as humans. We can learn to: walk, talk, play football, ride a unicycle, dance, drive, play a musical instrument, play chess or learn a language. **We continue to learn new things, with practice, throughout our lives!** We can develop new high-speed connections – whether it's learning a new skill or forming a new good habit.

When we have practised over and over, we can do some things without even thinking. You might not need to think at all about how you walk or talk – it comes naturally because you've had lots of practice! What new things have you already learned that took lots of practice and come easily now? Jot them down in the space on the next page.

★   Things I have already learned to do:

....

....

....

....

....

....

This means that we can always learn new skills!

Our brain is like a muscle – the things we practise cause areas of our brain to grow new connections. Lots of practice helps us learn new skills.

If you want to learn new ways to cope with difficult emotions, keep practising your new coping strategy (like the ones in Chapter 1) until it becomes a habit and you do it without thinking.

Remember!

- Your brain can learn all sorts of new things.
- Your brain changes throughout your life.
- This means that you keep learning new skills throughout your whole life.
- If you want to learn new ways to calm strong emotions, practise your skills over and over. This will make the connections you need to support change.

★   New things that I want to learn by practising:

....

....

....

....

....

....

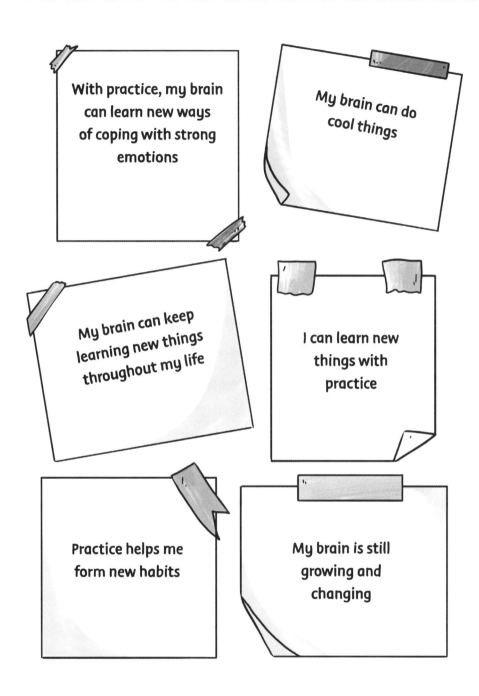

CHAPTER 11

Living With Strong Emotions

Emotions

scared content
sad rage excited depressed
jealous joyful guilty irritated worried
anxious peaceful calm ecstatic exhausted upset
disgust fearful angry rejected
proud overwhelmed

We all have a wide range of emotions. Life mostly teaches us to think that some emotions are positive (happy is seen as 'good') and some are negative or 'bad' (like anger or sadness).

★ In a moment, we will think about whether there is a better way of thinking about emotions, but first list below which emotions you have learned to think of as 'good' and which as 'bad'.

'Good' emotions	'Bad' emotions
....	....
....	....
....	....
....	....
....	....

Because some emotions are painful and seen as bad, people often try to change or get rid of them. When a big feeling comes along, like anger or sadness, you might also feel scared and overwhelmed by it, thinking 'Ahh I can't cope with this, I need to stop feeling like this, NOW!' This urgency to make the feeling go away causes even more stress. You may even start to panic about having the feeling in the first place!

Also, when we try to push down thoughts or emotions or try to not think about them, it can sometimes make them stronger. For example, if I ask you to stop thinking about a pink elephant...what do you picture in your mind?

Can you think of any emotions that you try to get rid of, change or push away?

★   Emotions that I try to change/get rid of:

. . . .

. . . .

. . . .

What do you do to get rid of them? You might do more than one thing.

★   I try to get rid of them by:

. . . .

. . . .

. . . .

People try to do this in lots of unhelpful ways, including:

- zoning out/numbing
- drinking alcohol
- taking illegal substances
- using self-harm
- distracting with romantic relationships.

These can become learned ways of trying to change difficult feelings in adults too. If we do any of these things enough, they can become a habit, which causes more problems than the feeling itself!

Imagine you have a friend, Sally (aged 21). Every time Sally has an upsetting memory, she drinks alcohol to forget how it makes her feel. It might feel better at first, but after a while, it could cause her lots of other problems. She might start being late for work, arrive tired from the night before or stop turning up at all. Buying the alcohol might use up a lot of the money she works hard for. Eventually, all this might cause problems in her friendships and relationships. After a while, Sally might find that the alcohol is more of a problem then the feelings she is trying to escape.

Trying to change or get rid of feelings can seem like an easier option at first, but often it causes more problems in the long term.

★   Are there any ways you try to change emotions that could be unhelpful to you over time? If so, use the space below to jot them down.

Strategies that cause me problems:

....

....

....

So, if labelling emotions as good and bad isn't the best plan, and escaping from them isn't either, what might work better?

A different way to think about it is that **all emotions** are natural to experience. We will have lots of different feelings, even in a single day.

We might feel:

- excited to go to the cinema
- nervous about meeting a new friend who is coming
- sad about an argument with a sibling while getting ready
- worried about a test at school next week.

And all this might be in one evening!

Changes in your emotions are normal and part of being human. Learning to notice and accept emotions without changing them takes time. This could be noticing 'I'm feeling sad now' and not trying to get rid of the emotion straight away. This can help you not to feel frightened by emotions. So, your new way of thinking about emotions could be aiming to accept all of them – without trying to change them or make them go away.

Allowing in difficult feelings – turning towards them instead of turning away – can be helpful. For example, feeling sad might help us think about what's causing this and how we can make changes in our life for the better. A wise young person once recognized that if they didn't feel boredom, they probably wouldn't experience excitement in the same way. They noticed that they needed one to feel the other, because if they felt excitement all the time, eventually that would get boring!

If we don't try to change the feeling (like sadness or anger), what do we do with it? One thing to remember is that difficult feelings don't last forever. It can feel overwhelming when we are sad or angry, so remind yourself that:

- difficult emotions pass
- you are not your feelings – the feeling is just passing through you and you are bigger than the feeling.

We can think of this as **riding the wave**.

Riding the wave

Visualize the emotion as the wave, and picture yourself surfing along with the water rather than trying to hold it back. The crest or peak of the wave will eventually break, and the energy will spread across the shore. Emotions, like waves, build, feel very strong and powerful, and rise and fall throughout the day. Practise riding the wave until it safely passes. This means accepting the feeling without trying to change it. If you tried to swim against a strong wave in the sea, would this work?

1. Accept the emotion.
2. Wait for it to pass.
3. Don't force it away.

This can be hard to learn, and you'll need people to help you practise your surfing!

★   Who can help you practise surfing and what situations could you practise it in?

....

....

....

Situations I can practise riding the wave in:

. . . .

. . . .

. . . .

Who can help me?

. . . .

. . . .

. . . .

Breaking it down

If you're not sure what's causing a feeling, break it down using the pie below. If you have a number of things happening, decide how big a slice you would give to each thing causing you stress. Here's an example for: 'I feel overwhelmed':

Feeling overwhelmed

Too much school work

Missing my brother

Worries about changing class

Argument with friend

Use this to think about how to problem solve or get support for the areas that are troubling you.

★ WHAT'S DRIVING MY EMOTION?

When you want to think about what's driving an emotion, draw your own version in the empty circle below.

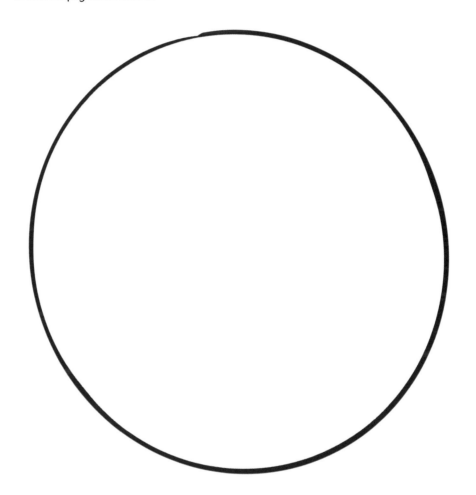

Strong emotions and life events

Strong emotions are usually related to life events, like feeling very sad when we have lost someone we love or angry when something unfair happens.

If you are reading this journal, you may have been through tough things, like: traumatic experiences, separations from people you love or having to move a lot. These events would make people feel a range of strong emotions, such as sadness, anger, anxiety or fear.

★   Mark which of the situations have happened to you on the list below.

☐ Separation from a parent
☐ Separation from a sibling
☐ Being hurt by someone caring for me
☐ Having to move between people caring for me
☐ Being in frightening situations with adults
☐ Frequent shouting/arguing between adults at home
☐ Not having as much care as children need
☐ Other experiences that have been difficult for me:

....

....

....

....

....

....

These events are especially hard to deal with when they happen to children, as there is no way that a child could be ready to cope with them.

If you are struggling with strong emotions, be kind to yourself. Remember that it might be because of things that happened in the past, but this doesn't mean things will be difficult forever. Emotions change over time and so can how you cope with them.

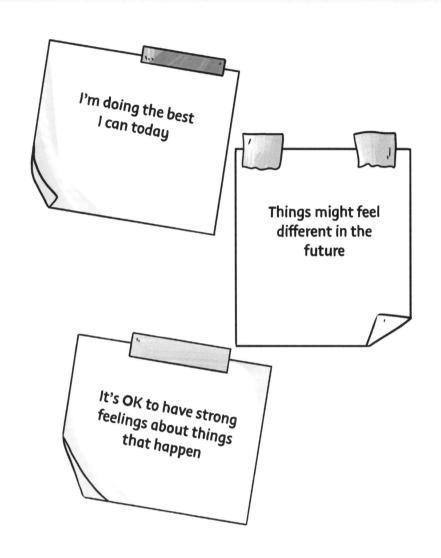

CHAPTER 12

Emotions and Attachment

This chapter talks about ideas that we looked at in Chapter 9 on attachment, so you might want to work through that chapter first. This section is about how attachment relates to emotions. Our parents or carers help us learn to cope with emotions. Very young children, especially babies, feel emotions very strongly and are not yet able to keep them in balance. What you might notice is that they are often either laughing or crying when they are awake.

Let's think back to the baby we talked about in Chapter 9. In the first house we looked at, if our baby was hungry, the parent would show they knew what he needed ('You must be hungry'), fix the problem (by feeding him) and comfort him to let him know everything would be OK.

The parent helped our baby in house one by:

- feeding him
- connecting the feeling in his tummy with the word 'hunger' – over time, this helps baby have words for feelings in his body
- helping him manage his upset about being hungry by using a soothing voice, rocking and cuddling him
- letting him know he will feel better soon – that food is coming.

Baby learns that this hunger isn't nice but it doesn't last forever, and adults can be trusted to make things better. He starts to find out that problems get better and difficult emotions pass over time. In this way, his parents **co-manage** his earliest emotions.

Remember!

- Emotions are managed with someone else when we are babies and toddlers.

- Once we can do this with someone else, we slowly learn that we are able to cope with our emotions and can calm ourselves down.
- This is how we learn to cope with difficult feelings – learning to ride the wave!

When co-managing feelings has been missed

In house number four in Chapter 9, our baby might have had a really different experience. He might not have had the messages that things get better, upsetting emotions don't last forever and problems can be fixed. In this house, he didn't have someone to co-manage his first big feelings.

If co-managing emotions doesn't happen often enough when children are young, it can be harder to learn to self-manage big emotions as they get older.

This can mean that emotions are felt very strongly or feel frightening and out of control. It might feel like they are never going to get better. It might feel like:

- sadness is felt intensely as **despair**
- worry is felt as **intense fear**
- anger is felt as **rage**.

Self-managing big emotions can be extra hard when you're a teenager, because people might start to say you're 'old enough' to manage emotions (without knowing about your earlier experiences). When emotions go outside the manageable range, fight, flight and freeze can happen.

If you are reading this journal, you might have experienced:

- more difficult life events, which can lead to more feelings of sadness, upset or anger
- less help co-managing difficult feelings earlier in life.

This doesn't mean you will always find managing emotions hard; it just means you might need to spend more time learning to ride the wave with the support of people you trust now! Let's go into more depth about some of the big emotions and think about what might help. Here goes...

CHAPTER 13

Anger

I just sometimes get really angry about little things. My foster carer asks me why I'm so angry but I don't know and I can't remember what I said after. Then I feel guilty for shouting at her. **Lucy, 15**

You might have had lots of things happen that could cause feelings of anger. It's totally valid that some experiences can lead to strong feelings of anger. Over time, these feelings can build up, like pressure building in a bottle, and then all it takes is a little shake and...whoosh...the lid comes flying off. The focus of this chapter is how to **feel it, not deal it**.

'Dealing it' is what you don't want to happen, because it causes more problems than you had before. If a teacher saying you don't have the right clothes for PE is the final shake of the bottle and the lid comes flying off – ending up with you shouting at the teacher – things will probably get worse, not better! The aim is to notice how you feel, understand it and let it come out in a way that doesn't cause you more problems. Make sense?

Think about a fizzy bottle of lemonade that's been shaken up. How do you stop the spray going everywhere when you open it?

- Time – wait for the pressure to go down before opening it.
- Let the air out a bit at a time.

Bottled-up anger

If it wasn't safe to express feelings of anger, you may have learnt to deny them. Let the pressure out now by gradually finding ways to safely express anger that don't hurt you or others.

★   I could express anger safely by:

....

....

....

It's hard to think clearly when we are overwhelmed by strong emotions. Really big feelings trigger fight, flight and freeze kicking in, and that makes wise owl from Chapter 10 go offline! This means we may do or say things that owl wouldn't usually allow. Anger motivates action. It gives you a lot of energy, especially in your arms and legs (which is why people might lash out when angry). If you've read Chapter 10 on fight, flight and freeze, you already know about this stuff.

Anger vs aggression

Everyone feels anger sometimes. Anger is different from aggression, which is acting out angry feelings.

★   Use the space below to write down situations that leave you angry and consider how strongly you feel the anger – give it an anger rating out of 10.

Situation	Anger rating
....	....
....	....
....	....

Internalized anger

Some people keep anger in but find it gets directed towards themselves – through hurting themselves or denying themselves nice things. If this is the case, this chapter is for you too – learning to express some of this anger safely rather than keeping it all in is important!

What helps?

Anything that calms the body and brain and gets owl back in charge will be helpful.

Acknowledge that you feel angry first. Try to understand it and accept it instead of pushing it out or changing it quickly.

Bottling up anger may work for a little while, but the anger is likely to pop up again (like a jack-in-the-box) when something else comes along. The more you push it down, the more likely it is to pop up when you are not expecting it.

Of course, you don't want to get stuck feeling angry for a long time, but give yourself a few minutes to feel it without trying to make it go away. This can be helpful with all emotions – allow them to be there (even if they don't feel nice), make space for them or ride the wave until the energy has passed.

Anger creates energy in the body through adrenaline, which prepares you for fight, flight and freeze, so find a safe way to release this. Exercise can really help to release adrenaline, and it helps our body to feel more relaxed. You can exercise in your room without equipment by doing star jumps, jogging on the spot or jumping up and down. Doing this for 10–15 minutes burns off excess energy, leaving you more relaxed. Exercise also releases serotonin – a chemical in your body which is thought to be important in balancing mood. It is often called the body's natural 'feel good' chemical.

Remember!

- Accept the emotion and that it's OK to be angry.
- Know how it feels and what your body does when you're angry.
- Ride it out – it won't last forever. You may need strategies to release energy that don't cause damage to you, to someone else or to any important things, like using a punchbag, or ripping up newspaper/old tights.
- Remember the lemonade bottle – let out the pressure a bit at a time; don't let things build up.
- For the long term, work out how to express these feelings through talking, exercise, drawing or painting.
- Feel it, don't deal it. Avoid acting it out to yourself or others as aggression.
- Problem solve situations that create feelings of anger.

Externalizing anger

You are not the feeling of anger. Anger is like the weather in the sky – the sky is always there, but the weather comes and goes. Storm clouds might come and then pass after a while, but the sky is still there. You are bigger than your emotion, and emotions like anger will come for a while then pass.

★   To help think of anger in this way (as not being the whole of you), you could write, draw, paint or graffiti anger in the spaces below.

What does the anger look like?

What colour would it be?

How big is it?

What shape would it be?

What would you call it if it had a name?

What does it feel like? Is it spiky? Hard? Rough? Smooth?

What makes it grow? What makes it shrink?

How do you know when it is making an appearance?

What can other people do to help you when the anger comes along?

Anger looks like:

★ ANGER: HOW IT APPEARS IN MY LIFE

About me	True	False
When I get angry, I try to push the feeling out	☐	☐
I try to push feelings of anger down	☐	☐
When I get angry, it comes out as aggression	☐	☐
When I get angry, I try to change my feeling using things that don't help me	☐	☐
I am learning to tolerate feelings of anger, even if it's difficult	☐	☐
When I feel angry, I can express what I feel in a safe way	☐	☐
I know who I can talk to if I feel angry	☐	☐

Things I'm going to try that help with anger	Tried?	Helpful?
Acknowledging feelings of anger	☐	☐
Reminding myself that feelings of anger won't last forever	☐	☐
Riding the wave	☐	☐
Doing intense exercise for 10–15 minutes (jogging on the spot)	☐	☐
Talking it through with someone I trust	☐	☐
Externalizing anger	☐	☐

CHAPTER 14

Worry

Feeling some worry is completely normal. It is part of being human.

★ You can use the clouds below to write down some of your biggest worries (some of the clouds might feel bigger or heavier than others):

When and where do you notice your worries?

- In the daytime.
- At school.
- At home.
- At night time.

We might worry about things that have happened, things in the future or even things that may never happen. Some people worry about things like: joining a new team, meeting new people, taking a test or reading aloud in class. This is completely normal.

★   Use the space below to note down three situations that you worry about:

1. ....
    ....
    ....
    ....
    ....
    ....

2. ....
    ....
    ....
    ....
    ....
    ....

3. ....
    ....
    ....
    ....
    ....
    ....

Worry can spur us on to do things we need to. If Mike has an exam at the end of the month, some worry might give him the motivation to revise. It might sound like 'What if I don't do well in this exam, what if I don't get the marks I need?' His thoughts might come with bodily feelings, like his heart beating faster and butterflies in his stomach.

If the worry prompts him to get his books out, it might be helpful in keeping him on track with his goal. But if Mike is overcome with fear every day and finds he can't eat or sleep, that would not be so useful!

A little bit of worry about things we can do something about can be helpful.

★ Use the space below to note down feelings and thoughts connected to the worry in the three situations you identified.

Situation	Body feelings	Thoughts
1.		
2.		
3.		

Worries might not be pleasant, but they are only a problem when they:

- get in the way of life often
- stop you doing things you want or need to do
- are around all the time and you can't switch off from them.

Worries about social situations or performing (like speaking in class) are quite common. These can set off judgy thoughts, like 'I'm not good enough', 'People won't like me', 'People will laugh at me' or 'I'll say the wrong thing.'

It might seem like you are on your own with this, but here's a secret: lots of other people are anxious, even if they don't seem it. Other young people might be worrying about lots of the same things as you. Thinking 'I'm not OK but everyone else is' can contribute to feeling stressed or different.

> Nala (15) was anxious about speaking in bigger groups and socializing. She talked to her friend Alexi, who was in the second year of uni, as she knew she'd had some anxiety but had overcome it.
>
> Nala: I get really worried about speaking in a group; it makes me feel sick. My throat goes dry and my heart goes so fast. I imagine the words will come out funny, I'll say something stupid and everyone will laugh. I've started avoiding lunchtimes so I don't have to see people.
>
> Alexi: I used to feel the same; it was awful. I wasn't going out because I was getting so nervous. I felt down when I was just stuck in my room. In the end, I decided things couldn't stay like that – I needed to make friends at uni and get out there.
>
> Nala: I'm starting to feel a bit lonely but can't get past the anxiety. What did you do? You seem really confident now.
>
> Alexi: I started pushing myself to mix, even if I didn't want to. Anxiety was telling me to stay in my room, but I thought – if I did that, how would it ever get better? So I started doing little things, like inviting one person for a coffee, then building up from there. I was nervous at first but I tried to focus on what the person was saying instead of on my anxiety. It helped, and after a while I was able to forget about anxiety because I was interested in what they were saying.
>
> Nala: Can you do big groups now?
>
> Alexi: I still get a bit nervous, but yes, I've learnt that even when I do get anxious, if I focus on who I'm with and what they're saying, it passes after a while. If anxiety crops up, I remind myself it will pass. It took practice but I can go out now without it bothering me much at all.

When the thing you are anxious about can't hurt you (like sitting an exam or reading aloud in class), the best thing is to do more of it, not less. You'll learn that nothing bad will happen, anxiety can't harm your body and it passes over time.

It's so tempting to avoid the things we worry about, but this can make the worries grow.

> **Note**
> This is different if the thing we are worried about can hurt us. In this section, we are only talking about things that make us anxious but are not actually unsafe and therefore can't hurt us.

Heavier worries

Sometimes I really worry about my mum. My social worker says it's not my job to worry about her, she's got support, but I can't help it.
Ryan, 14

You might have some worries that lots of teenagers have, like:

- worry about exams
- worry about starting a new club
- worry about friendship problems
- worry about appearance.

But you might also have some worries that are more serious than some other people your age.

- Is my mum OK?
- Where are my sisters living?
- What if we move again?

These worries can be heavier to carry. When carrying something heavy, it sometimes helps to put it down and take a break or to let someone help you carry the load. When you have heavier worries:

- be kind to yourself
- allow yourself breaks from worrying – when can you put the heavy worries down?
- let someone help you carry them.

Who is the person that can carry some of these heavier worries with you? It might be a carer, a support worker or someone at school. Part of self-care is letting people help you when you need it.

★   When I need help with big worries, I will:

....

....

....

....

....

....

....

....

....

Panic

Panic attacks can happen when we feel the anxiety is too much for our body to cope with.

Sometimes, anxiety can make people worry that it will cause physical harm to their body. Anxious thoughts can tell people:

- 'My heart is beating so fast – it might burst.'
- 'I'm so anxious – I might pass out.'

Anxiety feels unpleasant, but it can't hurt my body.

Anxiety feels unpleasant, but it can't physically hurt you. Thinking that anxiety could hurt your body would cause even more stress and keep the problem going! Remember, 'Anxiety might not feel nice, but it can't hurt my body.'

Anxiety feels strong now, but I know it will pass.

When emotions get really big, remember that you have felt like this before and that it will pass. Use your coping statements when things feel overwhelming. You could keep these in your phone. The list on the next page gives examples you can use and space to write down your own.

★ COPING STATEMENTS

- I've felt like this before – it feels awful now, but it won't last forever.
- This feeling is horrible, but it will pass.
- I will remember to be kind to myself when things feel bad.
- I am bigger than my emotions.
- I am not my emotion; my emotion just passes through me.

Use this space to write any other coping statements.

My statement 1:

. . . .

. . . .

. . . .

My statement 2:

. . . .

. . . .

. . . .

My statement 3:

. . . .

. . . .

. . . .

★ BUILDING MY SELF-CARE KIT

Build your self-care kit when you are feeling calm so it is ready for the day when things feel tough. You can use your senses to help calm you when you are feeling overwhelmed, so include things you like to see, hear, touch, taste and smell in your self-care box.

Example self-care kit

Hear: Favourite songs

Touch: Favourite fabric, bear, blanket

Smell: Lavender oils, favourite perfume

See: Drawings, pictures, happy memory photos

Taste: Bit of my favourite food/flavour

My self-care kit

Hear: ....

Touch: ....

Smell: ....

See: ....

Taste: ....

CHAPTER 15

Shame and Guilt

For a long time, I felt bad all the time. I felt like I must be an awful person and that if people knew, they wouldn't like me. I now know that was feelings of shame and that there is nothing wrong with me.
Kimi, 16

Shame and guilt aren't often talked about, so this section may feel weird! Let's start with what these strange emotions are and why we get them. Often, shame or guilt are around when we think we have:

- done something we shouldn't
- hurt someone
- disappointed someone important to us
- let someone down.

Weirdly, guilt is useful. It helps us think about our behaviour (because we feel for the other person, but also because we want to avoid the feeling in future!). This helps us learn and change.

When we are young, we need people to tell us when we are doing something dangerous or not good for us, like running into the road without looking or eating 10 chocolate bars in one go! A parent or carer would have to tell their child quickly and sharply if they needed to stop them running into the road.

Parents and carers help children learn when they've done something they shouldn't. For example, saying Freddie (6) can't hit his friend Sammy (5) for playing with Freddie's toy.

Hopefully, parents let children know that the behaviour is not OK but they still love them. These messages go together – 'You shouldn't have done that – don't do it again' with the reassurance of 'I still love you' (even if that bit is unsaid). When children are told what they did wrong in a way that is firm but shows love, it helps them learn what to do next time and how to get along with other people.

Guilt is helpful, so what's wrong with shame?

Shame feels different to guilt. It's bigger than guilt and it's hard to think when shame is around.

Shame gets stuck if children get the message that they as a person are the problem, not the thing they did. This can happen if parents are very critical a lot of the time or when they manage their child's behaviour through hitting, telling them they are bad or calling them names. If this happens regularly, children learn 'It is me that is bad, not my behaviour.'

Guilt = feeling bad about what we did.

Shame = feeling bad about who we are.

While guilt is manageable and helps us think about how we can change our behaviour, shame is different. It's an overwhelming emotion that people don't want to feel. Their reaction might be 'Yuk, this feels horrid', so they push it away by:

- saying they didn't do it: 'It wasn't me!'
- getting angry (because shame makes really strong feelings)
- avoiding thinking about it at all.

If children grow up with lots of shame, it can cause a feeling of 'I'm bad' like Kimi described at the start of the chapter.

This big feeling can easily be set off. It might be a teacher saying something about a child's behaviour, which triggers a big shame response, leading to anger, denial or blame, which might make the teacher feel very confused!

What helps?

First, ask: 'Is shame around? Is this why I'm feeling so upset or angry?' Remember not to let shame creep in – it can make it harder to access your compassion or soothing system (from Chapter 6), meaning you're less likely to be kind to yourself.

When you're calmer, ask: 'If I could get shame to stop being so hard on me, is there anything I'd be able to learn from this situation?'

Remind yourself: 'Even if I get told about my behaviour, that doesn't mean I'm not a good person. I can get told off in class, argue with a friend, make a mistake and still be a good person. Mistakes don't define me. I remember I'm good enough and can learn from them.'

Tell your trusted adult when shame is around and see if they can help you move it to guilt. For example, they might reassure you: 'You need to do your detention, but we love you and it'll be OK.'

★ **MY EXPERIENCES OF SHAME AND GUILT**

When I was younger, how did my parent/carer let me know that I had done something they didn't want me to do?

....
....
....
....
....
....
....
....
....

I mostly experience:

☐ Shame
☐ Guilt

Who can help me reduce feelings of shame and how would I like them to help?

....
....
....
....
....
....
....
....
....

CHAPTER 16

Bullying Thoughts

Thoughts

Thoughts are really important to emotional wellbeing. It's easy to let bullying thoughts take over – your own thoughts can become your worst enemy! They could sound something like:

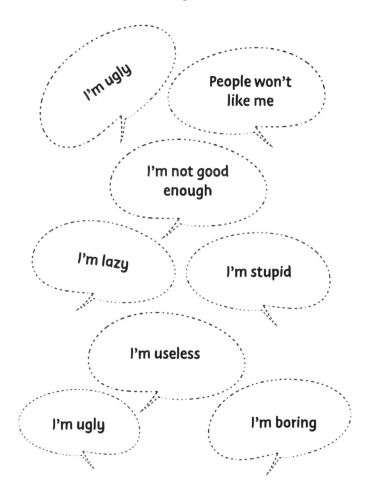

★ MY BULLYING THOUGHTS

If you get bullying thoughts, use the page below to record what these are.

Thoughts and why they matter

This section is based on ideas from Cognitive Behaviour Therapy (CBT). We will just use the foundations of CBT to look at thoughts, feelings and how we behave. These three areas all affect each other, so changing thoughts or behaviour can change how you feel.

Our emotions link to what we think and do. Let's imagine a situation.

Situation: You are walking down the street. You see your friend and she puts earphones in and keeps on walking with her head down. If you thought 'She's ignored me', you might feel upset or annoyed. And next time you saw her, you might ignore her and keep walking. The initial thought made you feel and do something.

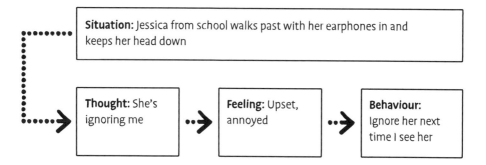

Now, let's imagine the same situation, but change the thought. So this time, you think 'She looks a bit distracted – I wonder if she's OK.' That might lead to feeling concerned about her and asking 'Hi, how are you today?' How you feel and the outcome for the friendship might be quite different.

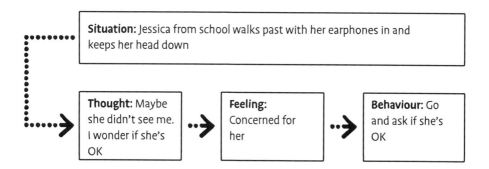

How people think might depend on what's happened in their life and what they've learned to expect. If people have been unkind often, they might automatically think it's happening again in a new situation. This can make meeting new people hard, for example, expecting that people can't be trusted or you'll get hurt. These **automatic thoughts** can happen quickly without you even noticing.

★   Use the boxes below to examine a situation that has bothered you. Work through what you thought, how you felt and what you did next. You can use the second set of boxes to explore other possible thoughts and feelings.

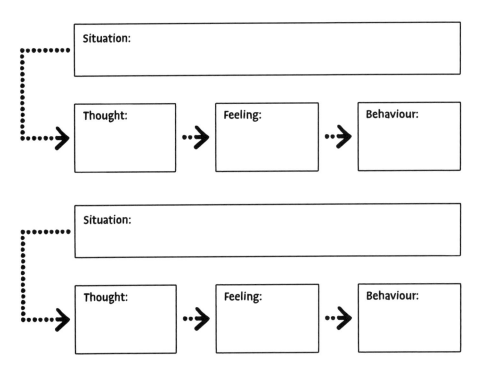

Random thought fact: 85% of what we worry about never happens! And for the 15% of worries that do happen, we find out we can handle it better than we expected 79% of the time!

Types of thinking
There are types of thinking that everyone can get stuck in that can increase feelings of sadness or worry. Here are some examples – see if you recognize any of them.

Predicting the future

This is all about assuming things are going to go wrong in the future. This might feel more likely if things have been challenging in the past, and it can be a way of trying to plan for what might go wrong. However, often when people predict the future, they focus on imagining things going wrong or failure, which can get in the way of trying something new.

This creates lots of 'what if?' questions, when in reality, no one can predict the future and trying to do so causes more worry. Think about whether these predictions leave you more or less worried: 'I won't get the grades I need to go to the college I want to', 'If I join a club, no one will speak to me and then I'll quit.'

If your mind jumps to future predictions, either let them drift in and out or offer yourself a different view, like 'Well actually I might join that club and make a really great new friend!'

Mind reading

This is about imagining you can guess what other people are thinking about you. When this happens, how often do you imagine they are thinking nice things? Especially if you've have had difficult early relationships, you might be more likely to imagine that people are thinking not nice things about you. But in reality, how can you know this?

Grey lenses

Have you heard the saying 'rose-tinted glasses'? It's used when people see things in an overly positive way. Well, the opposite of this might be 'grey lenses'. Grey lenses could be seeing the worst outcomes, picturing the downside of things or thinking things will be bad. This can evolve as self-protection, like 'If I don't expect good things, I won't be disappointed.'

Ignoring positives about yourself

This could be not taking a compliment, not noticing you got a good score on a test or not remembering you told a joke that made someone laugh. You might have a strong shield against letting in good news about yourself!

You might get a compliment and think 'Well, they have to say that' or 'They're just being nice', which can stop you really hearing it. If you don't let yourself hear compliments, you miss out on balanced information about yourself.

Instead, catch the positives! Practise noticing when something has gone well, when someone said something kind to you or when you laughed with a friend. Write these down and keep them in your jar – this makes them harder to ignore.

Catching thoughts

Some thoughts are deeply held beliefs about ourselves based on our relationships and experiences. Others flit through our minds so quickly we don't even notice!

Because some race through your mind so fast, it can be hard to understand how they make you feel. To understand this, slow them down to look at them more closely. Lots of negative thoughts about yourself can really affect how you feel.

You can learn to challenge bullying thoughts. First, imagine catching bullying thoughts about yourself, and then write them down.

★   Over the next 24 hours, keep a note of bullying thoughts that race through your mind. Let's start with catching five bullying thoughts:

Thought 1:

. . . .

Thought 2:

. . . .

Thought 3:

. . . .

Thought 4:

. . . .

Thought 5:

. . . .

Now we have caught five thoughts, let's take a look at them. Next to each thought, write whether it is helpful or unhelpful to you, and if it's unhelpful, how much upset it causes (out of 10).

Thought	Helpful/unhelpful	Upset caused/10
1.	. . . .	. . . .
2.	. . . .	. . . .
3.	. . . .	. . . .
4.	. . . .	. . . .
5.	. . . .	. . . .

When you can look at your thoughts and question them, their power goes down.

Questioning thoughts: Thoughts are not facts, they are opinions. But because they are your own opinions, they feel like facts. Weird, hey?!

You can learn to **challenge thoughts** instead of just believing they are true without looking at the evidence for or against them.

★ CBT AND ME

How much do I believe that my thoughts about myself are facts? (Circle the one that applies)

1   2   3   4   5   6   7   8   9   10

How much do I believe that my thoughts about myself are opinions? (Circle)

1   2   3   4   5   6   7   8   9   10

Testing out thoughts

Let's practise with a negative thought about yourself. For example, 'I am a bad person.'

The negative thought about myself is:

....

....

....

....

....

....

....

....

....

....

....

....

Before testing out this thought about yourself, let's consider how much you really believe it is true. One way to do this is to rate it out of 10 (where 10 = 'I totally believe it is true – no doubt!'). Next to the thought you just wrote down, write a rating out of 10 for how much you believe that to be true.

Next, we can view this thought in a balanced way and see if that rating might change. A quick example is below.

Example: I am a bad person

Evidence for	Evidence against
• It was said to me in an argument • I feel like it's true	• I helped my friend when she was upset about her boyfriend • I'm just as good as anyone else • I stuck up for someone in my class who was being picked on • I look after my hamster

★ Now try the same with your thought:

Evidence for	Evidence against

Now let's rerate your original thought. After looking at the evidence, how much do you now believe this thought?

You might notice that after doing this, you believe the bullying thought a little less. Even if it's gone down a point or two, that's a start! You can learn to do this for all bullying thoughts. Practise and see if it helps. Why not get someone you trust to practise it themselves with their own bullying thoughts!

> It's important not to just accept negative thoughts about ourselves as automatically true.

Best friend to myself

If it's hard to be kind to yourself, it might be easier to do it for a friend. Imagine…if your best friend was feeling this way, **what would you say to your best friend?**

If your best friend said they were 'boring' or 'no one cares about me', what might you say to them? Next time you are having these thoughts, consider what you would say to them, and then be just as kind to yourself. Practise learning to be your own best friend!

★ If you were being your own best friend, what three kind things would you say to yourself?

1. ....

2. ....

3. ....

Where are you spending your time?

Think about where you are spending most time in your thoughts. People might spend time in the present, past or future.

Sometimes, when people are sad, they might be lost in memories of the past. They might be spending so much time mentally in the **past** that they miss good things in the **present**.

When we are anxious, we might spend more time in the **future**, thinking things like 'Will I enjoy that party?', 'What if people laugh at what I wear?', 'What if that test goes badly?', 'What if that person never likes me?'

Often, when we spend time in the future, it involves dwelling on potential bad outcomes or thinking about what could go wrong. If we spend too much time in the future, we miss out on being fully in the present. This may mean that we can't focus on something good happening in that moment.

★   Consider your own thoughts and use the line below to mark:

- where you are spending the most time
- where you are spending the least time
- where you might want to spend more of your time.

Past   **Present**   **Future**

It's OK to visit the past or future in your thoughts, as long as you don't spend too long there and miss what's happening in your present!

★   So, we've talked about a few styles of thinking that can get stuck. Have a look at the list below to see if there are any you want to work on.

Thinking style:

☐ Trying to predict the future
☐ Mind reading
☐ Grey lenses
☐ Discounting positives
☐ Spending too much time in the past in my thoughts
☐ Spending too much time in the future in my thoughts

What helps?
Let's get back to bullying thoughts. Here are some good ways to deal with them:

- **Put thoughts in their place**: Remind yourself that's all they are – **thoughts**!
- **Instead of thinking 'I'm lazy', tell yourself**: 'No, I'm having the thought "I'm lazy" but that doesn't make it true.' This is the same

for all bullying thoughts. Remind yourself: 'I'm just having the thought that I'm useless/boring/stupid. That doesn't make it true!'

- **Questioning**: Is it really true? Remind yourself of other ways of seeing the situation. For example, instead of 'I'm lazy', you could think 'No one is perfect', 'I might need a rest today', 'I revised yesterday and it's Saturday today.'

- **Choices**: Notice when bullying thoughts are happening; write them down and notice how they make you feel. If a thought makes you hurt, shamed or upset, what might you want to do with it? You could rip up the paper, throw it away, question it or wait while it passes in your mind. You have choices – you don't have to just accept that thought as the 'truth' about you. Most thoughts will naturally pass quite quickly if we remind ourselves that they are just thoughts!

- **Not acting**: Remember, you don't have to act on every thought. If you have a thought like 'I'm bad', you can wait for it to pass without acting on it, especially if acting would be in a self-punishing way. Remind yourself:
  - it's just a thought
  - it doesn't mean it's true
  - it will pass.

- **Kindness**: When you get bullying thoughts, be kinder to yourself in response. Remind yourself of all the good things about yourself; check your compliments jar or go and talk to someone you trust.

- **Be your own best friend**: Practise being your own best friend. When it's hard to be kind to yourself, think of what you might say to a friend if they thought this about themselves.

- **I'm bigger than my thoughts**: Thoughts on their own can't hurt you if you remember that having them doesn't mean they are true.

★

THOUGHTS TABLE

Use the table below to find out more about thoughts, how they make you feel and how they influence what you do.

What happened (what was going on around me)	Thoughts	Feelings	What I did	Consequences (what happened next)

CHAPTER 17

Relationships (Getting an Updated Map!)

You are important to lots of people, in lots of ways.

★ If you have already completed the 'My relationships' exercise in Chapter 2 you can use this space to make a list of all the relationships you ticked.

My roles and relationships:

. . . .

. . . .

. . . .

. . . .

. . . .

These relationships will all be different. Each will make you feel different, and you might act differently in them all. You would be different in the role of a student (with a teacher) compared with the role of sibling.

Although these relationships are all different, we take a blueprint based on the past into new relationships. We might expect new people to fit into the same patterns as people we have known before and seek out people who behave in similar ways.

Thoughts, feelings and behaviours

We know that our thoughts are linked to how we feel and behave. And we know that what we expect to happen is linked to what has happened in the past.

For some people, their past leads them to believe that: new things will not go well, people are not good or people can't be trusted. It's easy to get into a cycle like the one below:

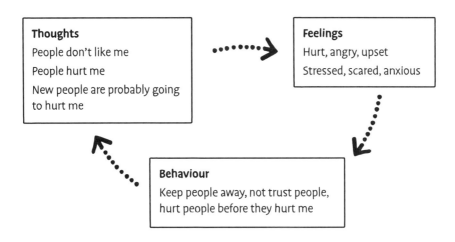

★ Use this space to write down what you have learned to expect from new people.

When I meet new people, I expect them to be:

....

....

I think that new people will treat me:

....

....

Because of this, when I meet new people I:

....

....

Friendships and romantic relationships

This chapter might help if you find yourself ending up with partners or friends who do not treat you well. If that is the case, continue reading this chapter.

I used to keep going for the wrong sort of person. If they treated me badly, I'd think it must be my fault and I'd try even harder to make it work. I'm trying now to pick someone who treats me really well, even though I still get insecure sometimes. **Joanna, 18**

Right, so remember we talked before about those stories you have about yourself? Well, if you have a story that goes something like... 'Once upon a time, there was a princess. She was great at everything and loved by everyone'... OK, not quite like that, but if you have a story a bit like that, you might expect good things and feel you deserve to meet someone really nice, kind, caring and cool! Why wouldn't you?!

But if your story about yourself is negative, you can end up not expecting people to be caring, and you may choose people who make you feel even worse! The problem is: this keeps that negative story going. The logic might then go something like: 'They aren't treating me well but I'm used to that, so if it's happening again, I must deserve it.' **Wrong!**

This view can keep you in bad relationships, where the situation happens again. Of course, when it's written down, it's clear that this isn't true.

Or it may be that you don't notice how you are being treated. If you've not been treated with kindness, you might not notice when someone new is being unkind, because their behaviour is familiar. You might not think 'They shouldn't have treated me like that' and you may be less likely to end the relationship if the behaviour doesn't seem unusual. And if someone is treating you well, thoughts like 'I don't deserve this' might crop up, leading you to push the relationship away.

So, have high expectations for how you want to be treated in a relationship! And high expectations about how you will treat the other person too, which is just as important!

The first thing might be to think: **How do I want to be treated? How would I know if someone was caring towards me – what might I see?**

It could be things like being:

- being considerate
- being kind
- being calm
- being gentle
- not putting me in dangerous situations
- encouraging me to do well in school
- valuing what is important to me – my interests
- taking time to get to know me

- not pushing me into things I don't want to do
- being polite to my friends/family
- remembering things I like
- paying attention to what I say
- remembering my birthday
- not being overly critical
- accepting me for who I am
- respecting when I say no.

If you have recently started a relationship, see how many of the ideas in the list you can tick and think about your own ideas below. What else might show that this is a good relationship for you?

★   How would I know this is a good relationship for me?

....

....

....

....

Warning signs

There can be warning signs in a relationship. They might include things like:

- is harsh
- shouts at me
- hurts me
- puts me in dangerous situations
- tells me school/college doesn't matter
- never does what I want to do
- pushes me into things I don't want to do
- is unkind to my family or friends
- doesn't find out what I like
- doesn't listen to me
- forgets important things, like my birthday
- criticizes me
- wants me to change a lot about myself

- doesn't respect when I say no
- talks about me badly to other people
- laughs at me (when I'm not laughing too)
- calls me names like 'stupid' or 'ugly'
- doesn't care if they hurt my feelings
- doesn't seem interested in getting to know me.

No one is perfect – everyone does some of these things sometimes, but check, if you're experiencing them, whether the relationship is mostly like the first or second examples.

Hopefulness

Even if you've had difficult early relationships, you can develop very safe relationships in future. If you notice yourself choosing people who don't value you and think this may be happening because of your previous experiences, here's how this can change:

First, notice it and remember how you want to be treated. We all deserve to be treated well. Try to 'fake it till you make it!', so if you don't feel like you are worthy of being cared about, just pretend at first by looking out for the things in examples of a good relationship earlier in the chapter. You could also start by doing kind things for yourself, like: practising self-care, looking after your body and being your own best friend. This helps develop a view of 'I'm worth caring about.'

These ideas also apply to friendships. Being a good friend can take practice. Use the space on the next page to jot down what makes a good friend. You can use the page after that to note down how you can be a good friend to others.

★ A GOOD FRIEND

Likes me for who I am

Doesn't make me do things I don't want to do

Helps me to feel good about myself

Doesn't talk about me behind my back, tells me if I've upset them

★ BEING A GOOD FRIEND

I can be a good friend by:

★ DEBRIEF SO FAR

You're doing really well! Let's pause to think about all the new things you've found out, things you want to try and topics that brought up big feelings for you. Maybe chat this summary through with your trusted adult.

Summary of ideas so far:	Topics that brought up strong feelings:
Things I'd like to talk about with an important adult:	**New things to try:**

CHAPTER 18

Unsticking Memories

Level 1: Memories that frighten us

For this section, make sure to get your team on board. It's about trauma so the safest way to work on it is to get support from someone you trust.

Post-traumatic stress symptoms can develop when:

- something traumatic has happened to you
- you have seen something traumatic happen to someone else.

The event/s might have happened once, or lots of times.

Traumatic events are outside the 'normal experience'. A typical day might be filled with normal events, like: getting the bus, eating breakfast or watching TV. Traumatic events are different. They are hard to understand and to fit into our brain. If someone experiences a distressing event, their brain works very hard to make sense of (process) what happened.

Traumatic experiences don't always result in longer-term symptoms. Sometimes, the brain is able to work through what happened and find a way to process it. The person might still have lots of thoughts and feelings about the thing that happened, but feels like it's safely in the past where it can't hurt them. Usually this happens gradually after the event – over a few months.

When someone is unable to process an experience, their brain can get stuck trying to figure out what happened and why. This can cause the memory of the event to keep popping back up – unprocessed and in its raw form.

Packing and storing memories

Before we consider trauma memories, let's think about usual memories. Usual memories get packaged and processed (like in a factory). They don't stay in full detail (all the sights, sounds, colours and smells of the experience) – this would be too much for your brain! They get packaged into something more manageable before being stored away. Imagine that this is like a cupboard full of large boxes. When you get a new memory, you pack it away with other similar ones. So you might have a box of Christmas memories that holds all your Christmas days. If these have been calm, the box might have themes around turkey, presents and decorations. You can open this box if you want to remember Christmas.

So, memories change from being information that arrives through your eyes, ears and nose to bigger themes. You might have lots of boxes on the shelf of processed memories, like a 'holidays' box or boxes about more regular activities, like 'football practices'. Normal memories are processed and stored away, ready for you to take out and look at when you want to.

But trauma memories are harder to process and store. Imagine having to store something very large that is a strange shape and has jagged edges in your cupboard. It might be too big to go in a box and you might not be able to work out what shape it is, what to store it with or where it fits.

Traumatic memories feel like this. When people can't process and package them, they push them to the back of the cupboard, unboxed. These memories can feel too big, sharp or scary to touch, so they get pushed to the back and then the door is shut tight.

But because these memories are not stored away neatly, they spill out of the cupboard when you get other boxes down, or the door bursts open when you are not expecting it. These unprocessed memories come with all the sights, sounds and smells that were around when the memory was made. When the memory comes back, it feels like it is happening, RIGHT NOW, not in the past. Because they are not stored away neatly in our timeline, they can feel like they are happening NOW.

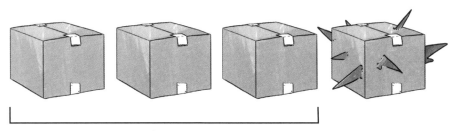

Typical memories   Traumatic memories

Aim: To be able to look at the memory, process it and store it. This helps get it in the right box and stops it falling out of the cupboard or popping up when you're not expecting it. If you had a cupboard to sort out, you wouldn't do it on your own, so make sure you ask for help.

> **Break!**
> Well done. You have covered a lot here so you might want a break. You can skip to the 'What helps?' section at the end of this chapter if you would like to, or you could spend 5–10 minutes using your grounding techniques from the 'My present moment' page in Chapter 1. If you want to learn more about trauma memories, continue on to Level 2: The detailed download, but only after a break!

Level 2: The detailed download

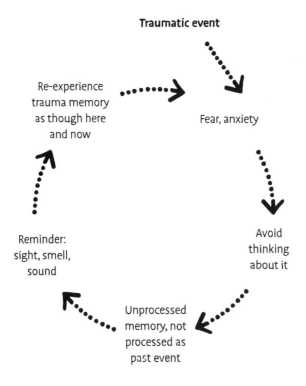

One of the things that can contribute to post-traumatic stress symptoms is really avoiding thinking about what happened. The brain doesn't get the chance to process it and it can leave the person believing they can't cope with thinking about it. It can feel like the memory is dangerous – like the event itself.

If the memory is avoided, the brain doesn't have time to process it and fit it alongside other memories. This keeps it isolated and it is not part of someone's whole story. While it is an isolated event – not part of the timeline – it remains **current** rather than a **memory of a past event**.

When the person is reminded of the event – by a sound, sight or smell – they might feel like they are back there and it's happening in the present. This is frightening, which means they try to push it back down and not think about it again. This cycle can continue, meaning they never get the chance to process what happened.

This type of remembering – where people feel they are back there and the event is happening again – is called a flashback. Flashbacks feel like reliving the event and include images, sounds and feelings that were present at the time. This can be frightening and anxiety provoking.

★ **PROCESSING MY MEMORIES**

At a time it feels safe to do so, you can use this page to think about how to work through memories that might be difficult for you. Write down how you want to start to safely process difficult memories and who can help you.

The place I feel safe to think about these memories is:

....

....

....

....

When I want to write/draw/paint my memory of the event, the person that I would like to support me is:

....

....

....

....

What happens in my body when these memories come along (heart rate, breathing, emotions)?

....

....

....

....

What memories do I get that I don't feel are under my control?

....

....

....

....

What do I do when the memory comes along (e.g., push it away)?

. . . .

. . . .

. . . .

. . . .

The thing I worry about if I let myself think about the memory is:

. . . .

. . . .

. . . .

. . . .

If I start to feel very distressed, I can do the following:
Examples:

- Connect with my safe person
- Slow down, take a break for a while
- Use things in my soothing box
- Grounding with the senses

- . . . .
- . . . .
- . . . .
- . . . .
- . . . .
- . . . .
- . . . .

Complex trauma

We've talked about post-traumatic stress symptoms, which can develop after one traumatic incident. For some people, traumatic events happen more regularly in the place they expect to feel safe (like home) and with people they are close to. When these things happen, more complex trauma can develop.

What is seen after complex trauma may have first developed as ways of coping with an unsafe environment, for example, learning not to trust others or to distance from the present.

Complex trauma is more likely to develop when:

- multiple traumatic things happened
- traumatic things happened early in life (as a child)
- traumatic things happened in a relationship with someone important to the person.

Chapter 4 explained that traumatic events can include things that happened, but also things that were needed but not there enough. This can include not having enough food, care, warmth, love and affection if they were absent a lot and over a long time.

People who have been through lots of traumatic events might notice emotional flashbacks (strong feelings they first felt at the time of the event/s). This could include fear, shame and sadness. Emotional flashbacks can cause someone to react to events in the present with the emotional strength felt in the past. This can make big emotions crop up that might be difficult for the person or others to understand.

When complex post-traumatic stress is around, people might notice things like:

Feelings of guilt or shame

Big ups and downs of emotions in a short time

Losing attention for a while/feeling disconnected

Relationship challenges, finding it hard to trust others

Taking risks with own safety

Frequent feelings of emptiness or hopelessness

What helps?
Setting safety
Traumatic memories can trigger very strong feelings. It's useful to make a plan of what you will do if you become very distressed while thinking about memories. Use Chapter 1 to remind yourself of your safety anchors for connecting to the present.

Processing memories safely
If avoiding thinking about frightening memories keeps the problem going, then allowing yourself to think about them in a safe way can help. Looking at memories when you feel calm helps your brain learn that the event happened in the past and is not happening now. Talking with someone you really trust, writing drawing or painting about it can help.

Managing flashbacks
Making your body feel safe first
The first thing to do is to get your body feeling that it is present and therefore safe. That sounds weird, right? But sometimes, if people are lost in memories, they can feel disconnected from their body, whilst their mind is elsewhere. One way to feel rooted in the present and in your body is through movement. This could be dance, yoga, walking or cycling. For some people, difficult memories come back most strongly when they are quiet and still, so movement can help. It also helps to discharge feelings of anxiety and fear.

Another option is to use your grounding skills. Feedback from the senses reminds your brain and body that you are not in the past. Ground yourself in the room you are in, for example: 'The chair is blue, I can see a tree through the window, I can feel the chair under my legs and the ground under my feet.' This helps bring you to the present, reminding your brain and body where you are now.

Coping statements
If you get flashbacks, write coping statements in advance. These might include: 'I know I am safe right now', 'This is a memory; I know it will pass.'

Understanding triggers
Understanding some of the reminders that trigger flashbacks can be helpful. This can help you feel more in control. Triggers can include sights, sounds or smells that were present at the time of the trauma. When these

naturally crop up in day-to-day life, they can take people back to the trauma memory. If you know in advance what these are, you can be prepared with your coping statements.

Updating the memory: what do I know now?

★ If you find yourself having flashbacks often, separate then and now by writing down what you thought would happen then (when the event happened) and what you know now.

What I **thought then**	**What I know now**
....	....
....	....
....	....
....	....
....	....
....	....
....	....

Creating distance from the memory

Remind yourself of the year that the memory happened and the year now, for example 'That was in X year when I lived in... Now it's Y year and I live in ...'. This might help your brain to 'update' to your current place and time.

You can create distance using language by saying 'I'm having the memory of...' rather than just feeling like it is happening now. This reminds your brain that it is a memory and not something happening in the present.

Safe image

What image would give you comfort if you visualized it when having a flashback? This is not a long-term strategy, as it is helpful to address the memories (rather than distract from or avoid them), but it can be helpful in the short term or if flashbacks feel overwhelming.

Or, if you have a distressing flashback, add into the image what a safe adult might say now, so you can imagine how they might have protected you when that image comes along.

★ **MY SAFE IMAGE**

Draw the safe image that will give you comfort here:

★ MY SAFE ADULT

My safe adult is: ....

If they had been there at the time, they might have done/said (draw or write):

Let's end this section with a metaphor for trauma

Imagine that the ball is the traumatic event and any subsequent symptoms. The jar represents everything else in the rest of life.

Focusing our energy on fighting the ball or trying to shrink it can be difficult and can leave people feeling tired, unsuccessful or hopeless if it doesn't work.

Another way of looking at it would be to acknowledge the ball, its size and why it's there, and then, instead of focusing on reducing the size of the ball, focusing on increasing the size of the life jar so the impact of the ball is less.

The rest of life includes all the fun stuff, which might be going to gigs, playing sport, being with friends, watching films, going on holiday, laughing with people and lots more! How could adults around you increase the size of your life jar? What different positive experiences might increase the width and depth of the jar?

Spend your energy increasing the size of the jar and while the ball won't disappear, it will naturally feel like it takes up a little less space over time.

CHAPTER 19

Survival Strategies

If you are in a situation where your body tells you there is danger, you may go into survival mode, like if you were in the army and under fire!

A survival strategy is anything that gets you through the scary time. In a conflict zone in the army, strategies to survive might include: wearing camouflage to blend in, crouching down and staying quiet and hidden. These would reduce the risk of attack and getting hurt. You might not be in the army, but if you have felt under threat in your normal life, your body and brain will have looked for ways to keep you safe.

When I was little, if things were bad, I'd go to my imaginary world in my head and talk to my friends there. It helped me to feel less scared. I spent less and less time with my imaginary friends after moving to my foster carer – I just didn't need them any more. **Aran, 14**

These imaginary friends helped Aran get through a tough time. Survival strategies are anything like that. They are ways you have adapted to feel safe. They develop over time to protect you from physical or emotional hurt.

When my uncle came round and was angry, I'd keep really quiet so that he didn't take it out on me. **Marty, 16**

My outer tortoise

One animal with good survival strategies is the tortoise! Let's think about him for a minute. He has a hard outer shell to keep things that might hurt him out. When he's scared, he pulls himself into his shell so he's fully protected. He keeps his softer, vulnerable parts (like his tummy) under-neath, where nothing can get to them.

★ Use the shapes on the tortoise's back to write down ways you protect yourself when you are feeling vulnerable.

How did you do with noticing your outer tortoise?

Some common tortoise/survival strategies are:

Survival strategy	What happens	Why it might happen
Hypervigilance (super-strength hearing and vision)	Staying on high alert to surroundings Not being able to relax Noticing every sight and sound	Developed in situations that were unsafe, where being aware of danger was important
Defensive anger	Always being ready to defend yourself, even when it might not be needed any more	Having been in unsafe situations where fight, flight and freeze was often triggered

Emotional scanning	Trying to read the emotions of others	To check whether everything is OK, to be ready in case mood of others changes
Controlling	Trying to stay in control all the time	Other people being in control may have not been safe Needing to be in control to care for self or others Not trusting adults to be in control
People pleasing	Overly pleasing others at expense of own wishes	If others are unhappy, they might hurt me/shout at me/get angry
Disconnecting	Shutting off, numbing – from people, relationships, feelings	Being present and connected has been too upsetting, painful or scary in the past
Overly independent	Not letting people take care of me, look after me or help me	It didn't go well in the past; people who were supposed to take care of me didn't

Some of these might be familiar or you might have thought of different ones. Let's look at emotional scanning and people pleasing as an example.

Emotional scanning might be something like noticing a change in expression on your friend Ben's face in a group conversation and your anxious brain saying:

Oh no, Ben is scowling, I wonder if he's OK.
Maybe I said the wrong thing. I wonder if he's mad at me?
What should I do to cheer him up?
How can I make him like me?

Exhausting, right?!

Emotional scanning might feel like 'I need to check how other people are feeling and monitor their expressions. If they're not happy, it must be something I've done' or 'If they're not happy, I should fix it, QUICK!'

And people pleasing is similar. It might sound like 'I must try to keep people happy all the time', 'If people aren't having fun, I must have done something wrong.'

So, if you notice this happening, try to turn down what your anxious brain is saying and let go of responsibility for how other people are feeling.

Downloading updates

Survival strategies are usually helpful at the time they developed. They might have kept you safe in a really unsafe place or time. But, what happens when you are in a place where you are now safe? Just like your computer, sometimes humans need to download updates too – and it can take time!

Let's imagine the guy from the army again. He's back home now, things are settled and he goes for dinner, but he's not yet updated his strategies, so he continues to crouch on the floor, wear his camouflage (including his face paint) and stay quiet and hidden under the table. The waiter and other diners might be very confused!

Survival strategies are useful when they are needed but might need an update when the situation changes. This can be easier said than done though, as things that kept us safe are hard to let go of. Survival mode can get stuck in the 'on' position, even when it's no longer needed.

What helps? Turning survival mode 'off'

If any of these things are still happening, consider whether they are still needed or not. If they still help you now, you might want to keep them; if not, start to let them go.

- Increasing feelings of safety in your life will reduce use of survival strategies. This might include having a safe person you trust and a safe place.
- Try to separate the here and now from the past, reminding yourself that your safety now is different from your safety in the past. If you find your brain keeps going back to the past, remind yourself that things are different now.

When I lived at home, I hated mum speaking to my teachers. If I'd been in trouble at school, that night would be worse at home. It was hard at first when my foster carer wanted to go into school for meetings. I'd be really worried when she got home, until I realized it was different here. **Caleb, 16**

★ Let's think about whether you notice yourself using any of these strategies and, if so, think about whether they are still useful or not.

Survival strategy	Do I show it?	If yes, do I still need it?	If I can let it go, where could I try this first/ who with?
Hypervigilance			
Defensive anger			
Emotional scanning			
Controlling			
People pleasing			
Disconnecting			
Overly independent			

If you notice some of these things going on, think about increasing feelings of safety generally. If you are emotional scanning and people pleasing, focus on both the wishes of others and your own wishes and needs. If you notice yourself disconnecting, use your grounding techniques and see if you can increase the amount of time you feel present, even when things are stressful.

It's really important to give yourself time when trying to make changes, do things differently or practise new skills. Remember what we said about our brains being capable of learning new things and experiencing things differently, but be aware that it will take time and practice for this change to become the new normal.

Come back to this section as often as you need to check out which strategies are still in use and which can have an update.

CHAPTER 20

School/College

For me, school was my safe place. I'd get given food at breakfast club and at lunch even if I didn't have any money. I'd go and sit in Miss Coulson's room and talk about things that were bothering me. **Mira, 18**

School might need a book of its own! Love it or hate it, school is important because it's where you probably spend five out of seven days. School might be tough or it might be a safe haven when other things are difficult.

★ MY EDUCATION

Let's think about your education, which parts you enjoy, what you find more challenging and what might help.

My school/college is called:

....

I am in Year:

....

This year in school, I hope to:

....
....

The subjects I like are:

....
....

The subjects I am best at are:

....
....

The subjects I find more difficult are:

....
....

My best friends at school are:

....
....

School has a mix of structured (lessons, assemblies) and unstructured (break, lunch) parts of the day. Some people like both parts of the day, whereas others prefer one or the other.

School has different important parts to it:

- social (friendships/clubs)
- learning (curriculum)
- behaviour (teachers, rules).

★ You might find some areas easier and others more difficult. You can use the space below to write down how you feel about each of these areas:

Social	Learning	Behaviour
....	....	....
....	....	....
....	....	....
....	....	....
....	....	....
....	....	....
....	....	....
....	....	....
....	....	....
....	....	....
....	....	....
....	....	....

Not many people find all three easy or have no problems in any of these areas. It's normal to find elements of school difficult at times. You might want to share what you've written with a trusted teacher so that they know what you need help with.

★ EDUCATION AND ME

What is school or college like for me?

....
....
....
....
....

What is difficult for me at school?

....
....
....
....
....

This is what I might be able to do to make school easier:

....
....
....
....
....

This is how other people can help me:

....
....
....
....
....

School when life is stressful

If things are or have been stressful at home, it can help to let someone trusted at school know. They can try to understand how you might be feeling and what might help. If you don't tell anyone, they can't help and might feel confused if they notice changes in your behaviour but don't know why.

> *School was hard. I didn't tell any of the teachers what was going on in my life. I was in trouble all the time or just sat there zoned out. They just thought I was being difficult and shouted a lot. I wish I had told someone how I was feeling.* **Lexie, 18**

Managing your inner meerkat

When people have been in stressful situations for a long time, they can find it hard to switch off from their environment. They might be super attentive to what's going on around them, so sounds or sights have them on alert!

At one time, this might have been really useful, like if there was often shouting at home, it would have been useful to be alert to what was going on to feel prepared.

The trouble is, at school, these super senses can stay turned on and tuned in to EVERYTHING that's going on around you, like someone coming into the room, the door slamming or unfamiliar sounds. And, of course, school is FULL OF SOUNDS! If there are 30 students all chatting, moving their chairs, opening pencil cases, you need to be able to tune some of this out. Being alert to every sound would feel overwhelming, making it hard to feel relaxed and ready to learn.

This can make some teenagers look distracted or jumpy. We might call this being **hypervigilant** to everything that is going on around them.

You might find you are the one in class who is alert and looking round to see what is going on – like the meerkat. This might be because your body is scanning for threats or danger, as though you are still unsafe.

A safe place to go to in school may help. The school will have a room for use when pupils are feeling stressed or overwhelmed. It can be helpful to have a safe person, like a teacher or member of the pastoral team, that you know well and trust. If it feels OK to do so, share some of your journal pages with them so they know the best way to help you.

Pop-up memories

In Chapter 18, we talked about memories that remain unprocessed at the back of the cupboard and how they can pop up again and feel like they are happening now. When things get loud in the classroom, what do teachers sometimes do to get heard over the 30 pupils? They shout! This might just be shouting to get heard, rather than shouting in anger, but it may bring back old memories of shouting. It might be hard to deal with in a full classroom.

> Sometimes it'd get really loud in class and Mr Simmons would start shouting. I couldn't help it but every time it'd bring back memories of the shouting at home – I'd get lost in that and forget I was at school and then get told off for not paying attention. **Max, 15**

If this happens, use the ideas on managing flashbacks in Chapter 18. If you've already talked to your teacher, agree a way to let them know if this happens. Of course, they can't see inside your mind, so letting them know what's happening is helpful for them and you.

Being told about behaviour

Right, so this is the job of every teacher, isn't it? Otherwise, things would get out of control pretty fast if everyone did whatever they wanted. Teachers might say things like 'Tuck your shirt in', 'Fix your tie', 'Why's your homework late?', 'No more talking' or 'You've got a detention'. They might say these things to keep everything running smoothly in class. But remember those stories we have about ourselves that we looked at in Chapter 5? If you've got one that says 'I'm pretty good, I make some mistakes but I'm generally a good person', it might be easier to cope when a teacher says you've done something wrong.

But if you've got a different story about yourself, one that goes 'I'm not good, people don't like me, I'm always in trouble', being told about these little things might feel much worse. It might feel unfair, like the teacher doesn't like you or is picking on you.

So, if you've had a difficult early start to your life, it can be hard to be told about behaviour (remember the part about shame and guilt). Remember we talked about rose-tinted glasses and grey lenses in Chapter 16? If you've had hard early experiences, it might be like wearing grey lenses, meaning taking on board feedback from teachers is harder.

What teachers say	Why they might say it	What grey lenses hear
Why haven't you done your homework?	Worried you might get behind	They always pick on me
You need to revise	Wanting you to get a good grade	They're criticizing me
No more talking	I can't hear myself think; how loud must it sound down the corridor? I need them to quieten down to teach the lesson	That teacher doesn't like me

It might not always seem like it, but teachers are people too. In a day, they could teach 30 students, five times a day. That's as many as 150 students per day!

Some days, they will be tired, frustrated or worried (sometimes about things like their students' grades). So sometimes, they'll be frazzled and less patient than normal.

Let's look at our thoughts. If your teacher tells you off for not handing in your homework, how you feel and react to this will depend on:

- your story about yourself
- the thoughts you get.

Let's think about an example from two points of view. Jenny (13) gets told off for not giving in her science homework. One way this could play out is:

Situation: Get told off for not giving in science homework

Story about herself: I'm usually pretty good – teachers usually like me

Thoughts: Mr Jones is telling me this because he wants me to get a good grade

Feelings: Feel a bit guilty

What she does: Does her homework next week

But, if Jenny's story about herself was different, it might change her thoughts and how she felt:

Situation: Get told off for not giving in science homework

Story about herself: People don't like me – I always get it wrong. I'm always told off

Thoughts: Mr Jones is telling me off because he doesn't like me; that's why he's picked on me

Feelings: Anger, shame

What she does: Shouts back, avoids his lesson next time

School summary
Difficulties that can happen in school

- Having strong emotions that feel hard to cope with, like anger, panic, anxiety and sadness.
- Getting flashbacks in school – feeling like I'm back in the past with unsafe things happening.
- Relationship difficulties/friendship issues.
- Difficulties concentrating and keeping focused due to feeling disconnected from bodily feelings or disconnected from the present.
- Fight, flight and freeze getting set off.

Things that can help

- Having a secure base in school – a place that feels safe.
- Letting a teacher or pastoral care worker know how things can be difficult and why – this can help you feel there is a safe person in school who understands you.
- Remembering that the pastoral team are there to help you. It's OK to ask them to listen, talk with you or help with solving practical problems.
- When things get tough, remembering your compassion statements.

- Remembering no one's perfect – it's OK to make mistakes.
- Having a sensory box that is kept in a safe place in school (see Chapter 1).
- If you need to calm, using your grounding techniques like 5, 4, 3, 2, 1 which is great because you can do it quietly in your mind (see Chapter 1).

CHAPTER 21

Being Assertive

When we are assertive, we show that our own needs **and** the needs of the other person are important. Sounds simple, right? But it can get a bit complicated. Let's find out what happens when we struggle to be assertive and why this might happen.

If you have been in relationships where your needs did not seem important, it might be hard to say what you need from others. Sometimes, people can end up not saying what their own needs are at all (being passive) or dominating others by pushing aggressively for what they want. If someone is passive too often, they might feel they never get what they want. If they are aggressive, the other person might feel this way, which could create arguments!

Being assertive is somewhere in the middle, where your own needs and the needs of the other person are important.

This can take time to learn! Let's look at some examples to find out more.

★ Let's have a go at sorting the three statements below into the list on the following page to decide if the response would be passive, assertive or aggressive. Use the blank spaces in each column to add them to the right list. Check your answers at the end of the journal.

1. Frightening others.

2. Finding it hard to say no.

3. Being calm and confident.

Passive	Assertive	Aggressive
• Don't say what I want • Put my own needs last • Do what anyone wants to avoid conflict • Give in to be nice • Feel powerless • Find it hard to set limits with others • Value self less than others •	• Firm • Clear • Fair • Express emotions • Both people's needs are important and respected • Making own choices • Value self and others equally •	• Using anger to get what you want or need • Using force • Controlling • Being physically aggressive • Hurting others • Attacking others. • Blaming • Value self more than others • . . . .

Now let's take a real situation and look at the possible responses.

Example situation: watching a film with a friend.

Let's use this example to look at what a passive, assertive and aggressive response might be.

Passive	Assertive	Aggressive
I never choose what film to watch when with a friend; I just let them pick and agree	Taking it in turns to choose a film each time we meet, compromising	I always get my way about the film we watch; if my friend asks for another film I shout until we watch mine

★ Now practise with this situation, sorting the possible responses into the columns, depending on where you think they fit. Check your answers at the end of the journal.

Situation: Your friends are planning on doing something that seems like it could end in trouble.

Possible responses:

1. Calmly saying you'd rather not do it and sticking to that.

2. Getting into a fight to get the group to do something else.

3. Doing it even though you don't want to because it's hard to say no, even though it'll get you into trouble.

Passive	Assertive	Aggressive

Being assertive involves being clear about what you want and saying this whilst also respecting what the other person wants.

★   Can you think of people in your life who have been passive, assertive or aggressive? Write down below what behaviour makes you think this about each person.

Passive	Assertive	Aggressive

★   Do you usually respond in a passive, assertive or aggressive way? Tick below:

☐ Passive
☐ Aggressive
☐ Assertive

Learning to be assertive takes practice! At first, it's not easy to move from dealing with situations passively or aggressively; it takes time.

★   Write down a situation where you want to be more assertive. What might you do next time that would help you to be more assertive?

Situation:

....

....

What will I do differently to be more assertive?

....

....

....

Sometimes, people hold views based on their experiences that keep them responding passively or aggressively. These can include:

Passive
- If I speak up, it will make other people angry if I don't agree with them.
- I don't deserve to ask for what I need.
- I'll make the wrong choice.
- I'm not as good as other people so I'll let them choose.
- No one will listen to me anyway.

Aggressive
- If I let other people have their way, I'll be walked all over.
- I can't trust people to be fair with me.
- It's not safe if I let other people make the decisions.
- People will think I'm weak if I don't appear strong and forceful.
- People will take advantage if they are not scared of me.

Part of learning to be more assertive is challenging thoughts that keep you stuck in passive or aggressive ways of responding.

You may have seen people who get their needs met by being aggressive or seen people who stayed safe by being very passive.

Think about role models – people you have seen who say what they want or need in a calm way while considering the needs of others. It could be a football coach, who isn't aggressive but people listen to them; it might be a teacher, a youth worker, a relative or a friend.

★ Use the space below to think about how you see them being assertive and any good results this gets, for example, the team playing well for the football coach.

Person	How do I know they are assertive?	What do they do that makes them assertive?	What good results do they get?

Can you use the table above to help your journey in learning to be assertive? Based on what you have thought about, what else might you do when being more assertive?

....

....

Another helpful tip for asserting your feelings or wishes is flipping a 'You' statement to an 'I' statement.

Sometimes, when we make comments that others might perceive as negative, they can become defensive and this can lead to arguments and breakdowns in communication, which no one wants! When we make 'You' statements, other people might feel like we're accusing them of something. Switching it up to an 'I' statement is a great alternative that means you can still communicate your needs, but you minimize the chance of the other person taking it badly.

Let's see what this could look like:

'You' statement
- 'You are being really unfair and always leave me out.'
- 'You need to stop talking about yourself all the time; it's so annoying.'
- 'You need to leave me alone.'

'I' statement
- 'I've noticed how much I miss your company; I feel like we used to hang out way more.'
- 'I'd like to tell you a bit about my day; I've got a lot on my mind right now.'
- 'I'm finding it difficult to talk at the moment...it would help if you can give me a bit of time to figure out how I'm feeling. I'll come to you when/if I need a chat.'

CHAPTER 22

My Present and Future

It might be that if you are reading this, some things have already changed a lot for the better.

★ Use the space below to write down things that have changed for the better or are going well.

The person/people I can trust the most now is/are:

....

I can tell that my parent/carer cares for me when:

....

....

The happiest memories I have made recently are:

....

....

What adults do to help me feel safe:

....

....

What adults can do that supports me:

....

....

★ SAFETY AT HOME

Hopefully, if you are reading this, you are now in a place that feels safe. Think about all the things that let you know your house is now safe. Some examples are given below, with spaces for you to fill in what you notice:

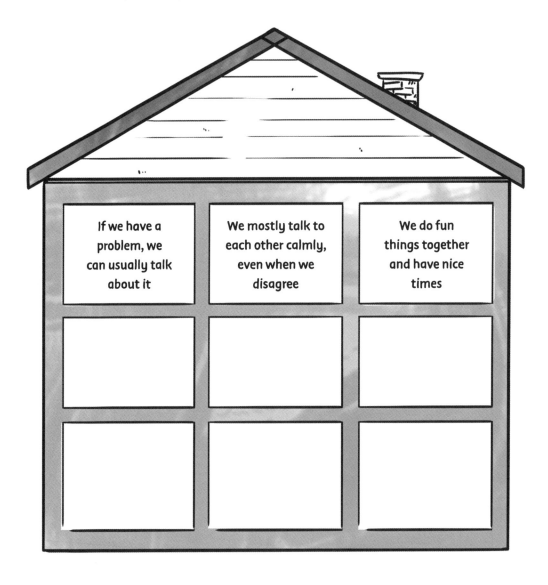

★ MY VALUED FUTURE

Even when the past has been difficult, the future can be different. Imagine yourself at 25. Think about: where might you be living, who will be with you, whether you will have any pets, what hobbies you might have, where you might be working. Write, draw or graffiti words or images of how you might want your future to look. You can return to this page when things are difficult to remind yourself of your valued future.

★ MY FUTURE – JOBS

There are so many options out there for the future and lots of exciting roles that you could have. Some jobs are listed below. If you've never heard of one before, maybe look it up to see if it's something you might be good at and enjoy. Whatever your strengths and interests, there's a job that would match them! Have a chat with adults around you about the list and your talents and interests.

Accountant
Architect
Artist
Actor
Baker
Barista
Business Owner
Barrister
Builder
Banker
Cleaner
Chef
Dentist
Carpenter
Dancer
Electrician
Engineer
Doctor
Decorator
Fireperson
Farmer
Gardener
Estate Agent
Florist
Interior Designer
Joiner
Poet
Nurse
Musician
Painter
Pharmacist
Photographer
Pilot
Psychologist
Police Officer
Plumber
Radiographer
Retailer
Recruiter
Post Person
Social Worker
Shopkeeper
Solicitor
Travel Agent
Sportsperson
Teacher
Waiter
Writer
Veterinary Nurse
Veterinary Doctor

★ **MY NEXT STEPS**

When you think about your future, what do you want in your life? What can adults do to help you with taking the next steps to get there? Use the footprints below to think about your next steps and how adults can support you with this.

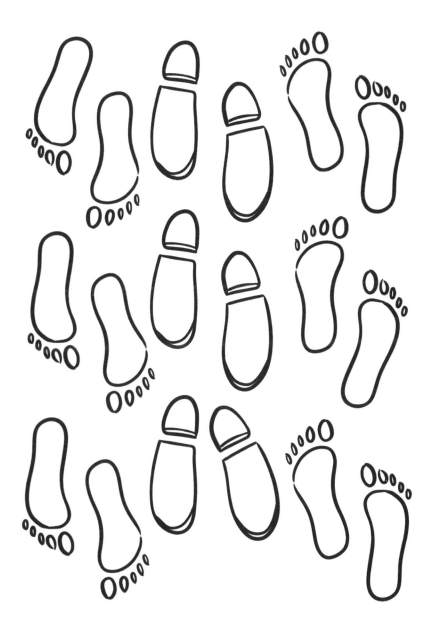

★ MY DREAMS

Think about your dreams and what your goals are. These can be big goals for life or smaller goals. The best way to approach goals is to break them down into smaller steps, working backwards. Ask yourself: 'If I want something in two years, what do I need to do next year, next month, tomorrow and even today to move towards this?' Goals can be social, academic, employment or achievement related – whatever is important to you. Moving towards goals in small steps can help you achieve your dreams! Taking the first step can be hard and we can put off starting, so use the space below to think about actions you can take as soon as today or tomorrow that will move you towards your dreams. You can continue thinking forward to what you might be doing next month or even next year to keep you moving towards your valued goals.

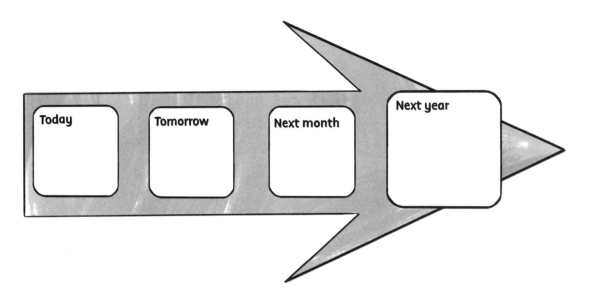

Today

Tomorrow

Next month

Next year

Summary

Thank you for working through this journal. I hope that some areas have been helpful to you.

Remember

Moving forward, be kind to yourself in the way you treat your body and the things you tell yourself. Taking care of yourself includes: looking after your body with enough sleep and exercise, having kinder stories about yourself and valuing yourself in relationships. All these things add up to feeling emotionally and physically well. Don't do these things alone; keep your support team with you for your next steps – we all need one. Having these foundations in place and the help of your support network will free you up to focus on the present and the amazing future you have ahead of you!

Well done, and remember you can download all the journal pages marked with ★ to use again at https://library.jkp.com/redeem using the code MZVSMRH

With warm wishes,

Laura

Help if You Need It

In Chapter 3, we said that being resilient is asking for help when you need it. So, if you need extra help, let your support team know so they can get in touch with a professional who can help. This could be going to visit your GP or speaking to your social worker (if you have one) or someone in school, as they will know about local support services in your area.

The details below are for national services that offer advice over the telephone or email. These are useful but not a substitute for getting support in your local area if you need it.

UK

Samaritans
Available 24 hours a day, 7 days a week, contact via telephone or email.
Telephone 116 123 (freephone)
Jo@samaritans.org

Childline
Telephone: 0800 1111

Young Minds
www.youngminds.org.uk

Kooth
www.kooth.com

USA

Lines for Life

Free, confidential, anonymous help in the USA, available 24/7.
Telephone: USA 800-273-8255

www.linesforlife.org

Australia

Lifeline

National charity providing 24/7 crisis support.
Text: 0477 13 11 14
Telephone: 13 11 14

www.lifeline.org.au

New Zealand

Samaritans NZ

24/7 crisis line.
Telephone: 0800 72 66 66

www.samaritans.org.nz

Remember, there are always people you can speak to if you need to.

Answers

★ **Chapter 10**

Owl	Lizard and Monkey
Doing my homework quietly	Shouting at my teacher
Choosing a film to watch from a list	Running off after an argument
Enjoying a chat with my friend	Slamming the car door after a row
Organizing a day out with friends	Throwing something in my room

Chapter 21

1. Frightening others. (Aggressive)
2. Finding it hard to say no. (Passive)
3. Being calm and confident. (Assertive)

1. Calmly saying you'd rather not do it and sticking to that. (Assertive)
2. Getting into a fight to get the group to do something else. (Aggressive)
3. Doing it even though you don't want to because it's hard to say no, even though it'll get you into trouble. (Passive)

Letter to Supportive Adults

Dear Parent, Carer or Guardian

If you bought this journal for an adolescent or teenager you know, that's great!

Relationships are central to this journal. The most important thing for anyone is a secure, caring relationship. If you are an adoptive parent, foster carer, special guardian or residential worker and bought this journal for a teenager, remember that the most important part of your teenager's healing is that they have someone close to help them.

There are wonderful writings on this already, including those by Daniel Hughes and Kim Golding. This journal doesn't repeat those ideas, as they are well outlined already, but they are central to this resource (I've included some recommended reading at the back of this journal if you are interested in finding out more).

If relationships are vital, it's important that this journal is a way to start a conversation. Your teenager will need to borrow some of your care and thinking skills to support them while reading this. It's recommended that you read through it first so you know what they will need and can discuss how they will let you know when they need your help.

The journal element of this book is for the teenager to record their own thoughts and experiences. I hope it will open new conversations about important topics and help deepen connections with those they are closest to.

With best wishes,

Laura

References and Further Reading for Parents, Carers and Professionals

If your parent or carer, a social worker or an adult from school has been helping you with this journal, they might be wondering about what else they could read. Here are some books and articles that relate to the ideas in this journal and what inspired them.

Caroline Archer (1999) *Next Steps in Parenting the Child Who Hurts: Tykes and Teens*. Jessica Kingsley Publishers.

Sally Donovan (2019) *The Unofficial Guide to Therapeutic Parenting: The Teen Years*. Jessica Kingsley Publishers.

Heather Geddes (2005) *Attachment in the Classroom: The Links Between Children's Early Experience, Emotional Wellbeing and Performance in School: A Practical Guide for Schools*. Worth Publishing.

Paul Gilbert (2010) *An Introduction to Compassion Focused Therapy in Cognitive Behaviour Therapy*. International Journal of Cognitive Therapy, 3 (2), 97–112.

Kim Golding and Daniel Hughes (2012) *Creating Loving Attachments: Parenting with PACE to Nurture Confidence and Security in the Troubled Child*. Jessica Kingsley Publishers.

Russ Harris (2008) *The Happiness Trap: Stop Struggling, Start Living*. Robinson.

Stephen C. Hayes (2005) *Get Out of Your Mind and Into Your Life: The New Acceptance and Commitment Therapy*. New Harbinger Publications.

Daniel Hughes (1998) *Building the Bonds of Attachment*. Rowman and Littlefield Publishers.

Sarah Naish (2018) *The A–Z of Therapeutic Parenting: Strategies and Solutions*. Jessica Kingsley Publishers.

Dan Siegel (2002) *The Developing Mind: First Edition. How Relationships and the Brain Interact to Shape Who We Are*. Guilford Press.

Miriam Silver (2013) *Attachment in Common Sense and Doodles: A Practical Guide*. Jessica Kingsley Publishers.

Dr. Karen Treisman (2017) *A Therapeutic Treasure Box for Working with Children and Adolescents with Developmental Trauma: Creative Techniques and Activities*. Jessica Kingsley Publishers.

Pete Walker (2013) *Complex PTSD, From Surviving to Thriving: A Guide and Map for Recovering from Childhood Trauma*. Azure Coyote.

Michael White and David Epston (1990) *Narrative Means to Therapeutic Ends*. W.W. Norton and Company.

Jon Kabat-Zinn (1994) *Wherever You Go, There You Are: Mindfulness Meditation for Everyday Life*. Hachette Books.

Care-experienced authors

There are some writings from people who have lived experience of being in care.

Lemn Sissay (2020) *My Name Is Why*. Canongate Books.

Hope Daniels and Morag Livingstone (2012) *Hackney Child. A True Story of Surviving Poverty and the Care System.* Livingstone Media.

Ben Ashcroft (2013) *Fifty-One Moves.* Waterside Press Ltd.

Acknowledgements

With extra special thanks to members of the Cumbria Children in Care Council (CICC) for reviewing and providing feedback on a draft. This feedback was so helpful in shaping the final journal; thank you to all the young people who contributed their time and brilliant ideas! Also thank you to Rebecca Barnes from CICC Cumbria for supporting this; it was so important to have the views of care-experienced young people, so your help was so appreciated.

I would like to acknowledge the amazing generosity of friends in helping to shape this journal – taking time to read drafts and sharing so many creative ideas. Thank you to Danielle and Ellen for that early conversation that made it seem possible. Big thanks to Faiza, Matthew, Claire and Ellen for honest feedback and creative ideas when I was being concrete! Particular thanks to Ellen for co-authoring Chapter 4, which was a very helpful addition.

Thank you to all the children, young people, families, foster carers and adoptive parents I have worked with over the years. I have learned so much from you all.

With thanks to Stephen Jones, Carys Homer and everyone at Jessica Kingsley Publishers for their ideas, knowledge and support with this project. Also thanks to Masha Pimas for the excellent illustrations which help to bring the words to life.

Matthew, thank you for the unfailing support and patience, especially at weekends!

Importantly, thank you from the bottom of my heart to Julia and Michael, always, for their constant love, teaching, support and encouragement.

About the Author

Dr. Laura Stokes is a Consultant Clinical Psychologist who works in the National Health Service (NHS) with children and families. Laura worked with looked-after and adopted children, young people and their families when she first qualified.

Dr. Ellen Westwood co-authored Chapter 4 and is also a Clinical Psychologist working in the NHS. Ellen has experience working with children, young people and families, as well as with adults experiencing issues relating to homelessness.